W9-CBF-391

847839

794.2 Wiswell, Thomas.
WIS
        The wonderful world
        of checkers and
        draughts

DATE		
NOV 1 1 1995		
NOV 1 1 1995		
NOV 22 1996		
DEC 0 3 1996		
SEP 2 6 1997		
NOV 1 0 1997		
NOV 2 0 1997		
JAN 2 9 1998		

WITHDRAWN

The Wonderful World
of Checkers and Draughts

Also by TOM WISWELL:

Let's Play Checkers
Learn Checkers Fast
America's Best Checkers
Checkers in Ten Lessons
Checker Magic
Challenge of Checkers and Chess
Checker Kings in Action
The Art of Checkers
International Draughts
Twentieth Century Checkers
Championship Checkers and Chess for All
The Complete Guide to Checkers
Secrets of Checkerboard Strategy
The Science of Checkers and Draughts
Top Notch Checkers (Co-author)
Chess (with Kenneth Grover)

Also by JULES LEOPOLD:

Checkers—Secrets of the Experts
Modern Checkers (recorded on cassette)
Check Your Wits
At Ease!—200 Hours of Fun and Entertainment
Test Yourself
How to Solve Rebus Puzzles
How to Solve Number Path Puzzles
Techniques of Puzzle-Solving
Positional Word Lists for Puzzle Solvers

The Wonderful World of Checkers and Draughts

Tom Wiswell *and* Jules Leopold

SAN DIEGO • NEW YORK
A. S. BARNES & COMPANY, INC.
IN LONDON:
THE TANTIVY PRESS

The Wonderful World of Checkers and Draughts
copyright © 1980 by A. S. Barnes and Co., Inc.

First Edition
Manufactured in the United States of America

For information write to:

A. S. Barnes & Company, Inc.
P.O. Box 3051
La Jolla, California 92038

The Tantivy Press
Magdalen House
136-148 Tooley Street
London, SE1 2TT, England

Library of Congress Cataloging in Publication Data

Wiswell, Thomas.
  The wonderful world of checkers and draughts.

  Includes index.
  1. Checkers. 2. Checkers—Collections of games.
I. Leopold, Jules, 1912-   joint author. II. Title.
GV1463.W55   794.2   78-69631
ISBN 0-498-02258-7

1 2 3 4 5 6 7 . 8 9   84   83   82   81   80

I will therefore take occasion to assert that the higher powers of the reflective intellect are more decidedly and more usefully tasked by the unostentatious game of Draughts than by all the elaborate frivolity of Chess. In the latter, where the pieces have different and bizarre motions, with various and variable values, what is only complex is mistaken (a not unusual error) for what is profound.

—Edgar Allan Poe (*Murders in the Rue Morgue*)

Contents

Acknowledgments

The authors wish to thank the American Checker Federation and its officials for their consideration in granting permission for use of some official tourney play in this book.

We also wish to express our gratitude to all of the players whose names appear among the problems and games herein. Without their lively participation in Checkers many interesting facets may not have yet been brought to light.

Some of these players are among the many who have made the Chess and Checker Club of New York their favorite Draughts dueling ground. Within its heady atmosphere many an intriguing game developed, and many a beautiful problem took root. The Club has been in existence for over fifty years. Among its perennial visitors is the veteran expert, Rosario DiLorenzo, who is now in his nineties. Time has not diminished his zeal and enthusiasm for the game.

Also—though their names are not shown among the problems and games in this volume—we want to express our appreciation for the contributions made by John Cary, Ernest Churchill, Roland Heathcote, Parks Herzog, James Keene, Tom Landry, Anthony Petronella, Herb Richter, Bill Salot, Dr. Lewis Schreiber, Joe Schwartz, Antonio Tammaro, and Louis Van Deven.

Our grateful appreciation extends to all who contribute to the lore and love of the game. This includes the officials and district officers of all Checker and Draughts associations and the supporting members thereof. Few may be Checker champions but all are champions of Checkers!

The Wonderful World
of Checkers and Draughts

Introduction

Checkers (or, in England, Draughts) is a game of paradoxes—things are not always what they seem. To begin with, even its universal popularity conceals a remarkable paradox. For, while many people play *at* Checkers, few actually do play Checkers . . . the *real* game of Checkers.

Yes, there is a wonderful world of Checkers whose existence is not even suspected by the casual player because the pure simplicity of its facade makes him seek no further.

But, as Edgar Allan Poe observed, it is a mistake to suppose that the profound can come only from the complex. Everywhere around us there are examples of profundity deriving from simplicity.*

Once you realize this, you find no real paradox in the statement that the game of Checkers contains inexhaustible depths beneath a surface of utter simplicity. And the more you get to learn about the *real* game of Checkers, the more you appreciate the truth of this statement.

Truth is beauty, and the devotees of Checkers find beauty in the endless revelations that can be discovered in its depths.

To the uninitiated it may seem strange that anyone could find beauty in a game so unpretentious in appearance. Comparison is made between the modest clothing of Checkers and the regal panoply of Chess . . . and Checkers is relegated to the cracker barrel, as was Cinderella to the fireplace before her beauty was brought to light.

But, of course, beauty is not mere surface glamour; it comes from sources

---

*To cite but two examples: Only four elementary units are at the base of the genetic code that transmits all biological inheritance. Only two elementary states, coded as "zero" and "one," are at the base of the digital computer's amazing capabilities.

As for Checkers, only four elementary monads are at the base of endless combinatorial possibilities—the Black checker, the White checker, the Black king, and the White king.

within. This is just as true for Chess; its real delights lie not in its external splendor but in its inner depths. Those who know both games well cannot agree with Poe's characterization of Chess as "elaborate frivolity," although they readily concur when Poe extols Checkers for its neat elegance.

This book, in seeking to communicate the beauty of Checkers, is in the most literal sense a labor of love.

There has been, too, a division of labor between Tom Wiswell and myself, Jules Leopold.

Tom Wiswell devoted many months to selecting and compiling the exemplary group of one hundred problem positions which appear herein along with the games from which fifty of these arose. Among these problems are many of Wiswell's own famous compositions. Solutions are given, with instructive annotations by Wiswell. Also represented are a number of other distinguished problemists and players. I have added an occasional comment or variation of my own, including the introductory remarks that accompany the Problem pages.

One need not be in the expert class to have some awareness of the charming felicity of the solutions to these problems. In these, and in the conduct of the accompanying games, there is dramatic demonstration of how checker subtleties disport themselves across the board.

For the beginner, however, an even keener appreciation is certain if he has first acquired understanding of some important basic Checker ideas . . . so many of which recur, like thematic chords, in the Problems and Games. Moreover, after having attained familiarity with such primary concepts, the beginner will begin to notice a rapid improvement in his playing ability, marked by sharpened perception and judgment.

To these ends, enhancement of appreciation and of ability, I have sought to provide a palette of essential Checker ideas in the chapters that now follow. Included with this presentation of basic themes is a good deal of instructive guidance, expert advice, and illuminating comment. These chapters, I hope, will serve to introduce the newcomer to the world of true scientific Checkers—and to prepare him for the Problem and Game pages, in which that wonderful world of Checkers is further revealed.

ALSO—within the Index (*page 170 on*) I include page-number guides showing where basic themes can be seen in operation among the 100 Problems. I urge the reader to make fullest use of these.

A few brief Checker aphorisms appear beneath some of the problem solutions. These are offered by Tom Wiswell and myself in the hope that the reader will take them on faith, trusting that they are born of long experience. Some Checker oddities and perplexities are also noted. Many of these alone may serve to refute the notion still held by a few that Checkers is just a kid's game.

2 Easy Numbers

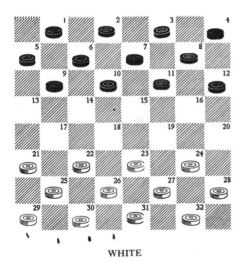

Note: For better clarity, this book (like most other checker books) reverses the colors of the squares in printing checkerboard diagrams. The dark (playing) squares are shown as white, and the nonplaying squares are shown as dark.

Do numbers leave you numb?

They shouldn't—at least not the kind of numbers you see in the notation of Checkers.

Checker numbers make it possible to report a game by presenting a serial record of the moves. Anyone who can count from 1 to 32 can immediately grasp the method of numbering the 32 playing squares, as shown.

Note the easy left-to-right sequence of the 32 numbers. By convention, at the start of each game, Black (who moves first) occupies squares 1 through 12, while White occupies 21 through 32. ("Black" and "White" are usually used as standard designations for the contrasting dark and light checkers, regard-

15

less of actual colors used. Most kindly to the eyes are red and white checkers placed on the green squares of a green and buff board, as employed in official matches and tournaments.)

To record a move (or jump) requires two numbers. The following brief example makes this immediately clear: 11-15, 22-18, 15-22, 25-18 . . . is a shorthand way of saying: Black moves from square 11 to square 15, then White moves from 22 to 18, then Black jumps from 15 to 22, then White jumps from 25 to 18.

With practice, one gets to know the numbered squares by heart. Unless you have already reached that stage of familiarity, be sure to number your board as shown. DO IT NOW . . . and keep your numbered board before you when following the moves given in this (and other) checker books.

There exists a popular belief that Checker numbers embody some arcane mathematical formula for calculating the best moves. Alas, there is absolutely no truth to this notion. The numbers do no more than provide a means for recording the moves.

3 Easy Rules

The rules of Checkers are given in many elementary books on the game, usually under the heading "Standard Laws of the Game." For the most part, these are so well known generally that I shall not devote space here to their formal presentation.

Instead, I will deal, informally, with those few aspects of the rules which may not be familiar to all.

BEGINNING. To begin, the players choose for sides. Black moves first; players alternate colors thereafter.

TOUCH IS MOVE. If you touch a piece, you must move it.* Furthermore, once having moved over the angle of a square the piece must complete its move in that direction.

If you touch a piece that you cannot or may not move, you are cautioned for the first offense—but the second offense is penalized by forfeiture of the game.

J'ADOUBE! This French phrase, or its English equivalent, "I adjust," is what you must *first* say if you want to touch a piece merely to adjust it. Then, no obligation or penalty.

JUMPS. All jumps and their resulting captures must be completed. That is, you can compel your opponent to jump and capture whenever such situation confronts him. If there exists more than one way, the player takes his choice.

Modern Checkers has eliminated the old "huff" rule which gave one the option of removing an opponent's checker for his failure to jump.

TIME! Unless the players have agreed otherwise, the "Time" rule is: When five minutes is up you get notice, and then you must move *before* the end of another minute. Change "five minutes" to "one minute" when you have a

---

*A touchy situation occurred in a Chess game when the nearsighted Steinitz touched his bishop with his nose. However, a kindly referee decided not to invoke this rule here. (The rule also applies to Chess.)

no-choice jump. Penalty for overtime is forfeiture of the game.

CROWNING. A single (uncrowned) checker can go forward only. But after it reaches the opposite king row to be crowned, it can thereafter go backward or forward. (Both, in case of certain multiple jumps.) To designate this extra power, the opponent must crown the new king immediately.

IN AND OUT. The act of becoming a king terminates that play. So, if a single checker upon jumping into the king row confronts *another* jump, it cannot take this "out" jump during the same (crowning) play. It must stop and allow the other side to move.

This rule makes possible a unique stratagem known as the "In and Out Shot." For a basic example, set up the following position on your board: Black on 21, kings on 6, 7, 14, and 15. White on 25, 30, 32, king on 31. White to move and win. Solution: White takes the "In and Out Shot" by 30-26, 21-30 (king, and stop!), 31-27, 30-23, removing all five Black kings in one fell swoop!—White had benefited by the "waiting move" he had obtained.

THE WIN. A curious omission in the "Standard Laws of the Game" is any definition of what constitutes a win! Probably because this was supposed to be automatically understood by all.

Yet one encounters occasional misunderstanding. A few people seem to believe that if a player is unable to move any of his pieces, the game is declared a draw. Not so!

In Checkers, the definition of what constitutes a win can be expressed in three simple words: LAST MOVE WINS.

Yes, the one who makes the last legal move wins. To win, you must run your opponent out of moves.

Usually, when a player can no longer move it is because all his checkers are gone. Sometimes, however, he can no longer move because whatever checkers he still has are "blocked" or "smothered."

Here are two examples in which Black loses because of the absolute immobility of all his remaining checkers:

a) Place Black on 19, king on 28. Place White on 27, king on 30. White to move and win.

Solution: 30-26, 28-32, 27-24, 19-28, 26-23, 32-27, 23-32. Black is blocked; since he cannot move, he loses.

b) Place Black on 17, 20, 21, 23, and kings on 30, 31. Place White on 25, 28, 29, 32. White to move and win.

Solution: 28-24, 20-27, 25-22, 17-26, 29-25, and Black is smothered. Although four checkers ahead, he loses because he is unable to move!

THE DRAW. It isn't as easy to define a draw as it is to define a win. Of course, a draw would be the verdict when both sides agree that neither can force a win and that further play would be futile exercise. When a draw is mutually accepted, play has usually reached the end-game stage with relatively few pieces remaining.

Some readers may wonder why an occasional game or problem solution appears to be abruptly concluded in print with the summary dismissal of "Draw"—when there surely is scope for additional play. The reason can be stated quite simply: Assuming normal care on both sides, neither can expect any further opportunity to win from that stage.

Of course, in actual play, one could continue hoping for an egregious blunder on his opponent's part. But the unwritten code of the checker expert precludes insisting upon "playing it out" until the bitter end just because of this very unlikely possibility. Such would be considered a waste of time, time more happily employed in starting a new game.

Nevertheless, if your opponent rejects your offer of a draw and insists on continuing what you deem fruitless play, you may invoke the 40-move rule. He then must show, to the satisfaction of a chosen qualified referee, that he has attained an increased advantage before the expiration of 40 additional moves on his side. (Once he does this, a new 40-move count may start.) Otherwise, the game is declared a draw.

4 What Every Checker Player Should Know

Checkers is a battle of ideas. You will see this vividly illustrated in the collection of one hundred problems and fifty games that is presented later on in these pages. Often the key to the required solution is an ingenious but elusive concept. Then there is revealed the sure logic for obtaining the desired result through forcing moves timed with precision.

As you follow the games and the problem solutions you will be intrigued by the revelations of so many different subtleties. But, besides providing entertainment, these revelations will surely gain for you an invaluable arsenal of ideas for your own crossboard encounters.

One purpose of the chapters that follow is to make sure that you are more fully prepared to receive these ideas. A background of certain Checker fundamentals is essential, both for that purpose and for increasing your playing skill. I shall proceed to discuss and explain these basics while you attend with numbered board and checkers.

But first let me reply to that often asked question: "What is the best move to start with?"—Here hindsight is better than foresight, we rely on the accumulated experience of the past rather than on "looking ahead."

Black has seven first-move choices, of varying strengths. The "strongest" may put White on the defensive, the "weakest" may put Black on the defensive. Yet each is viable. None permits a forced win for White . . . or for Black.

Here is an approximate comparison based on rating "strongest" as 10:

11-15(10)	9-14(9)	11-16(8)	10-15(6)
12-16(4)	10-14(4)	9-13(2)	

But remember, a "weaker" opening may prove effective against someone who is not experienced with it. Also, you get valuable crossboard exercise.

Next question: "What is White's best reply to each of Black's openers?" Well, to some there is one White move that is definitely best, to others there are fairly equal choices. Moreover, 22-18 is always safe, if not best.

The following listing shows the better White replies. After each, I continue play further to show one (of many) ways in which the game may develop.

<u>11-15, 23-19,</u> 8-11, 22-17, 4-8, 17-13, 15-18, 24-20, 11-15, 28-24, 8-11, 26-23, 9-14, 31-26, 6-9, 13-6, 2-9, 26-22, 1-6 (9-13 loses, 22-17, 13-22, 20-16, 11-20, 21-17, 14-21, 23-14, 10-17, 25-2).

<u>11-15, 23-19,</u> 8-11, 22-17, 11-16, 24-20, 16-23, 27-11, 7-16, 20-11, 3-7, 28-24, 7-16, 24-20, 16-19, 25-22.

<u>11-15, 23-18,</u> 8-11, 27-23, 4-8, 23-19, 10-14, 19-10, 14-23, 26-19, 7-14, 24-20, 6-10, 22-17, 9-13, 30-26.

<u>11-15, 22-18,</u> 15-22, 25-18, 8-11, 29-25, 4-8, 24-20, 10-15, 25-22, 12-16, 21-17 (27 or 28-24 loses, 15-19, 24-15, 16-19, 23-16, 9-14, 18-9, 11-25, any, 5-14).

<u>9-14, 22-17,</u> 11-15, 25-22, 8-11, 29-25, 11-16, 24-20, 16-19, 23-16, 12-19, 17-13, 4-8, 27-23, 8-12, 23-16.

<u>9-14, 22-18,</u> 5-9, 25-22, 11-16, 24-19, 8-11, 22-17, 9-13, 18-9, 13-22, 26-17, 6-22, 30-26, 11-15, 26-17.

<u>11-16, 22-18,</u> 8-11, 18-14, 9-18, 23-14, 10-17, 21-14, 4-8, 24-19, 16-23, 27-18, 12-16, 28-24, 8-12, 26-23.

<u>11-16, 24-19,</u> 8-11, 22-18, 4-8, 18-14, 9-18, 23-14, 10-17, 21-14, 16-23, 27-18, 12-16, 28-24, 8-12, 26-23.

<u>10-15, 21-17,</u> (best), 11-16, 17-13, 16-20, 22-18, 15-22, 25-18, 8-11, 29-25, 11-16, 25-21, 7-10, 26-22, 4-8.

<u>12-16, 24-20</u> (best), 8-12, 28-24, 3-8, 22-18, 16-19, 24-15, 10-19, 23-16, 12-19, 25-22, 9-14, 18-9, 5-14.

<u>10-14, 22-17,</u> 7-10, 17-13, 3-7, 25-22, 14-17, 21-14, 9-25, 29-22, 10-14, 22-18, 14-17, 24-19, 6-10, 27-24, 1-6, 19-15, 10-19, 24-15, 6-9 (12-16 loses, 15-10, 6-22, 13-9, 5-14, 23-18, 14-23, 26-3.)

<u>10-14, 24-19,</u> 6-10, 22-17, 11-15, 17-13, 15-24, 13-6, 2-9, 28-19, 8-11, 25-22, 11-15, 29-25, 15-24, 27-20.

<u>9-13, 22-18,</u> (best), 10-15, 25-22, 6-10, 23-19, 11-16, 18-11, 16-23, 27-11, 8-15, 18-11, 7-16, 22-18, 4-8.

ALSO, SEE GAMES on page 119, 122 to 127, 138 to 143, 156 to 160, 163, and 165.

5 The Corners and the Main Lines

Each player has two corners on his side. For obvious reasons, the square on your left-hand corner is called the Single Corner. The *two* playing squares that embrace your right-hand corner constitute the Double Corner. The same is true for your opponent. So there are two Single Corners, one is square 4 and the other is square 29. And there are two Double Corners, one being formed by squares 1 and 5, the other by Squares 32 and 28.

The diagonal line of squares that leads from one Single Corner to the other is called the Single-Corner Line. Each of the two lines that connect the opposite Double Corners is called a Double-Corner Line.

The Double Corner has a special virtue: it can be a haven of refuge for a king. That is to say, a king in a Double Corner cannot be captured by a lone pursuing king because the Double Corner provides room for perpetual seesawing.

But a king in a Single Corner, or in any border square other than a Double Corner, can be trapped there by an opposing king that has "the move." (The concept of "the move," or opposition, will be dealt with further on.)

It is important to realize that a king can reach a Double Corner only after first occupying a Double-Corner Line. Therefore, in a one-king against one-king finale, one king can force a win *only* if he is able to bar the other king from access to a Double-Corner Line.

A simple illustration: White king on 4, Black king on 29. White to move and win. Here White has the opposition, and simply by moving directly to confront can prevent any Black attempt to occupy a Double-Corner Line. After four of his moves, Black gets pinned to the wall.

With Black king on 29, there are 15 other squares (besides square 4) on which the White king can initially be placed to effect the win. Can you name all 15?

6 Power of a King

The added mobility that a checker gains by becoming an operable king translates into extra power. One mark of the expert is the ability to put that power to effective use.

There are many ways in which a king may be usefully employed. Basically, however, he is a potential threat to the security of any unidirectional enemy man, and may be in a position to capture or to force retreat into an untenable situation.

This may be perfectly obvious even to the rank beginner. Yet, often, he blithely disregards the obvious tactical implications.

For example: having succeeded in obtaining a first king, he immediately confines him to innocuous retirement. Instead of putting that royal power to immediate use, he keeps the king idle while he goes rushing out to obtain more kings. (Meanwhile, of course, his opponent keeps improving his own position.)

It is a fallacy, of course, to regard Checkers as a game that merely eventuates in a battle of kings. Once you have obtained the first king, it is usually wise to put his power to use as early as possible.

As with most generalizations in Checkers, this may occasionally be subject to discretionary exceptions. You may perhaps find that some other situation on the board requires more immediate attention.

7 The Corner Regions

In a general sense, the region near a Single Corner is intrinsically strong, the region near a Double Corner is intrinsically weak. The following simple demonstration will show why:

Set up the 24 pieces in the initial play position. Remove the four checkers from squares 4, 8, 11 and 12—Black's Single-Corner region. Now, see for youself how *difficult* it still is for White to enter Black's king row.

Next, try a similar removal in Black's Double-Corner region. Remove the checkers on 1, 5, 6, and 9. Now, see how *easy* it is for White to enter Black's king row.

From this we may conclude (apart from other factors that may be considered) that you can better afford to create open squares on your left (Single Corner) side, than on your right (Double Corner) side. In Tom Wiswell's pithy summary: "The player with a strong Double Corner is doubly hard to corner."

This is why the beginner is often told that a safe procedure is to confine his first three opening moves to 11-15 . . . 8-11 . . . 4-8 when playing Black.

8 Dyke Squares

One way, perhaps the more usual way, to prepare for an attack on your opponent's Double Corner is to post one of your checkers on his Dyke square. For White this means occupying square 14; for Black, square 19. Each of these squares represents an outpost to the opponent's Double Corner.

Why are these called Dyke squares? Because the usual intended strategy is to achieve the kind of line-up represented by pieces on 14, 18, and 23—suggestive of a wall, fence, or dike. (The variant spelling "dyke" is traditional in Checkers nomenclature.)

With such a line-up, a propitiously timed exchange by 14-9 (assuming Black has a checker on 5) may further harass the opposing Double Corner.

It is well to be alert to the Dyke idea, but it is a mistake to suppose that it represents an infallible method. You must respect your opponent, and in any given situation consider what counter resources he has.

Bear in mind then that a checker advanced into your opponent's territory can become a liability rather than a potent force, unless:

1. You first make sure that you have sufficient backing for that advanced checker to protect it against all opponent's possible attempts to capture it, and
2. That your necessary protective measures do not create a fatal weakness elsewhere on your side.

Accumulated experience with his own and with published master play enables the expert to distinguish a weak Dyke from a strong Dyke.

9 The Dog Hole

It is usually a poor idea for White to enter square 5 while Black still occupies square 1. Or, correspondingly, for Black to enter 28 while White occupies 32.

Such a move is called "going into the Dog Hole." It renders that checker immobile—well, at least until (if and when) the other side moves out of square 1 (or 32).

Here again, positional considerations may negate this advice. For example, you may enter the Dog Hole purposely because you can see that your opponent will soon be forced out of his Double Corner. Either by the factor of timing, or by a well-considered sacrifice on your part. Experience can tell you when it may be worth sacrificing a checker in order to get a king.

Another potential source of weakness, somewhat analogous to the Dog-Hole idea, may occur for White if he occupies 12 while Black is on 3, or correspondingly if Black occupies 21 while White is on 30. Here too, the checker is rendered somewhat immobile—and furthermore, may provide support for an opposing checker (on 16, or on 17, as the case may be).

Here also, considerations of timing and position may produce exceptions to the general rule.

10 One Up-Manship

To gain a checker is usually tantamount to winning the game, although there are many exceptions where positional factors dictate otherwise. In fact, some of the most beautiful themes in Checkers involve the deliberate sacrifice of one or more pieces as the only way to achieve the desired result. You will see many fine examples of this later among the one hundred problems.

The beginner, however, who blithely "gambles" on the sacrifice of a checker—in the hope that a kind fate will reward his generosity—has a mistaken notion of what the game is all about. Checkers should never be regarded as a game of chance.

Any plan to give away a checker must involve sure insight into what compensation or superiority will ensue—and this requires consideration of all the opponent's resources . . . including the possibility that he can counter-sacrifice with devastating effect.

The reality is that, while opportunities for ingenious valid sacrifices may occur often, these are the exception rather than the rule. Everything else being equal, the player who is definitely a man ahead needs only to conduct his afterplay with reasonable care to consummate his assured win.

Often this win can be completed simply through judicious (i.e., non-weakening) exchanges, until forces are reduced to an easily manageable few. The game may so resolve itself down to two kings against one. Here the Double Corner will prove no refuge for a lone king. Two opposing kings can drive him out, pin him to the edge of the board, and force submission.

The procedure is direct and simple, but many beginners fiddle around needlessly before homing in for the win. It should require no more than seven forcing moves from this position:

Black king on 1, White kings on 10 and 14. White moves 14-9, then 1-5,

27

10-14 (the key move), 5-1, 9-5, 1-6, 5-1, 6-2, 14-18, 2-7, 18-15, 7-2, 15-11. Done!

How to win with three kings against two kings is often an elusive problem for the novice. After floundering aimlessly he may have to abandon the position as drawn, especially if the opposing two kings have taken to opposite Double Corners. Such a state of affairs was dubbed "The Beginner's Jinx" by the late, great master William F. Ryan.

The trick is to reduce matters to two against one. Obviously this requires forcing an exchange. But there lies the difficulty for any novice who faces a cagey opponent.

Well, it's easy when you know how. The exchange can be forced, as the following will show:

Place Black kings on 9 and 27, White kings on 10, 15, and 19. White to move and win.

As each move is made, try to see why Black's replies are virtually forced in his efforts to avoid the inevitable exchange.

White moves 15-18, 9-5 (if 27-32, the procedure is the same but on the opposite side of the board), 10-6, 27-32, 19-23, 5-1, 6-9. Now Black has two choices, 1-5 or 32-28. Each leads to a key position.

If 1-5, White replies 9-14. This is one key position; note well the straight line-up.

If 32-28, White replies 23-27. This is the other key position; note well the staggered line-up.

After either key position, Black can no longer avoid an exchange. See for yourself.

Now return to the original position, but this time with Black to move. Black goes 9-5, then 15-18, 5-9, 10-14, 9-6, 19-23, 27-24, to bring about a mirror-image of our original White-to-move position. From here White's procedure is the same as shown.

Of course there are other positions involving three kings against two. In some, an exchange cannot be forced and other tactics are required to win. For example:

Black kings on 27 and 32, White kings on 15, 20, and 28. White to move and win.

White goes 15-19. This offers the two-for-one shot by 27-24, which Black refuses to take. (See why?) So Black replies 27-31. White then moves 20-24, forcing 32-27. Now it looks as if White has blundered, because if 24-20, then 27-24 gets Black a draw. But instead of 24-20 White moves 28-32. Then 27-20, 19-24, and White wins.

Another example: Black kings on 22 and 30, White kings on 13, 14 and 21. White moves 14-17, then 30-26, 21-25, 22-29, 17-22, and White wins.

How about four kings against three kings? If you have trouble forcing an exchange, look for this winning sacrifice idea:

Black kings on 30, 31 and 32, White kings on 20, 21, 22, and 24.

With White to play, 24-28, 31-27, then the sacrifice by 22-26, 30-23, followed by 28-24, wins. With Black to play, 32-27, 21-17, 27-32, 24-28, 31-27, then 22-26 is the same winning sacrifice.

11 When Two Will Not Beat One

There are a number of exceptional positions in which two checkers will *not* win against one. It is important that the beginner acquaint himself with these situations. There is no telling when, though a checker behind, you may be able to salvage your game by maneuvering your opponent into one of these endings.

Set up, each in turn, the positions indicated below. Absorb the ideas involved, making them part of your checker repertoire.

In each case, assume that you are playing White and that your last move has now placed you in the controlling position shown. In each it is Black's turn to move; although one ahead he cannot win. In fact, as you shall see, there are even a few such situations in which he cannot avoid losing!

Remember now—each position here is given as with BLACK TO MOVE while you are playing White.

1. Black king on 10 and 19, and White king on 15. White draws by "The Breeches." This can occur in many places on the board.
2. Black on 18, 19 and White king on 15. White can do no worse than draw . . . by "The Fork." This can occur in many places on the board.
3. Black kings on 29 and 30 (or 21), and White king on 22. Black moves 30-25. White replies 22-26 (or 22-17), thereafter always returning to 22. A perpetual draw. The same can occur, of course, at the opposite Single Corner.
4. Black on 5, king on 13, and White king on 14, Black moves 13-9, White replies 14-10 . . . repeat. Again, a draw by repetition.

Other examples of this are: Black on 13, king on 21, and White king on 22. Also, Black on 21, King on 29, and White king on 13 *or* 22 *or* 23 *or* 30. Also, Black on 12, king on 20, and White king on 19. Of course, if in such positions *both* of Black's men are uncrowned, White has at least a draw, and in two cases (find them!) White has a win!

5. Black on 14, king on 29 *or* 30, and White king on 22. Or, Black on 13, king on 30, and White king on 22. In either case, White can do no worse than draw.

6. Here are a few more related draw situations, each with one White king against two uncrowned Black checkers.
   —Black on 5, 6, and White king on 7 *or* 14.
   —Also, Black on 13, 14, and White king on 15 *or* 22.
   —Also, Black on 11, 12, and White king on 10 *or* 19.
   —Also, Black on 6, 9, and White king on 17.
   —Also, Black on 11, 16, and White king on 24.

7. As previously noted, there are certain positions where one side loses even though he has two to his opponent's one. Witness these; in each, though Black is one ahead, he must lose!
   —Black on 13, king on 29, and White king on 21 *or* 22.
   —Also, Black on 13, 21, and White king on 22.
   —Also, Black on 5, 13, and White king on 14.

8. Also, be alert for the following "pitch and squeeze" idea in which one side (here, White) deliberately reduces forces to his one against opponent's two in order to win!
   —Black on 18, 27, and White on 26, king on 28. Now, if Black should crown on 31, he would lose by 26-23!
   —Also, Black on 17, 26, and White on 25, king on 27. Should Black now crown on 30, he loses in the same fashion, by 25-22.
   —Also, the same idea can occur with Black on 19, 26 and White on 27, king on 25 . . . except that here Black cannot avoid losing in any case. (Note, however, that if you change the Black man on 26 to a king, Black *can* draw by 19-23 and "The Breeches.")

9. Now note this ending which White can win only by reducing his forces to one against two. Black on 16, 28 and White on 32, king on 26. Black moves 16-19, White replies 32-27! Black crowns, 28-32. Then 27-24, 19-28, 26-23, 32-27, 23-32, White wins by the "Block", as shown in the chapter, "Easy Rules."

If you think "it can't happen here," I offer evidence that it *can*, in the following classic problem. Here the terms are White to move and win. White can accomplish this only by forcing an ending in which he is left with one king against Black's two men.

Place Black men on 5, 9, 13 and king on 29. Place White men on 17, 22, 23 and king on 24. White to move and win.

Solution: 24-28, 29-25 (nothing else helps!), 17-14, and regardless of which sequence of jumps Black selects, White moves 28-32 to win . . . although a checker down!

12 Payne's Draw

There are a few notable endings in which three cannot beat two. The best known of these is "Payne's Draw." Place Black on 13, kings on 14 and 15. Place a White king on 22 and on 30. Black's turn to move.

If White handles his kings properly, Black finds himself unable to release his man on 13 and must eventually concede a draw. In general, White's defense is based upon controlling square 22 while keeping his kings in close cooperation.

In fact, it is Black who must be careful here. For if he allows vaunting ambition to overreach itself, he may fall into some trap that loses for him!

At the above position, with Black to move, an expert player invariably concedes the draw to an equally expert opponent, knowing that further play is futile.

The casual player, however, believes that with three checkers he should win here against two. And I know of one expert who, years ago, had converted this mistaken belief into a source of modest profit for himself. He would maneuver the innocent amateur into the majority side of Payne's Draw position and then invite a wager . . . a fair wager, since he would stipulate, "If it's a draw, nobody collects."

Nearly always *he* would collect. Few of his opponents could resist pressing determinedly for the (chimerical) win—and he did nothing to discourage such gung-ho enterprise. Almost invariably, then, they would wind up falling into any one of a number of possible losing traps.

Check these out for yourself:

TRAP no. 1:   14-17, 30-26, 15-19 . . . Black loses by 26-30.
TRAP no. 2:   15-19, 30-26, 19-24, 26-30, 24-27, 30-25, 14-17 . . . Black loses by 25-30.

TRAP no. 3: 14-17, 30-26, 15-10, 22-25, 10-14 . . . Black loses by 25-21.

TRAP no. 4: 14-17, 30-26, 17-21, 26-30, 15-19, 22-25, 19-23, 25-22, 21-17, 22-26 . . . and Black must allow the jump for a draw. More likely, however, Black will instinctively move the threatened king . . . and lose by 26-22.

TRAP no. 5: 14-17, 30-26, 17-21, 26-30, 15-10, 30-26, 10-14, 26-30, 14-17, 22-18 (*not* 30-26!). Now Black can still draw by 17-14, but few can resist the more inviting 17-22. Then, after White jumps 18-25, Black cannot avoid losing by the one-for-one exchange that White will next make.

Now you might ask, "Doesn't Black have any traps of his own?" Well, there is one subtle winning trap he might try for, with a remote possibility that White will be lured into it. A little applied psychology might help, as you shall see:

From the position; 14-18, 30-25, 18-14, 25-30 . . . *repeat* these moves a few times. By such repetition (whose purpose is that of the magician's device of misdirection) Black hopes to get White into the habit of moving 30-25.

If Black is successful in so habituating White, he can pull a rabbit out of his magician's hat—so:

14-18, 30-25, 18-14, 25-30, 14-9, 30-25, 15-10, 25-30, 10-6, 30-25 (bad habit! 30-26 is necessary here to draw), then 13-17, 22-13, 6-1, 13-6, 1-10, and Black wins.

13 The Factor of "The Move"

This is the most important concept in Checker end-game theory. For a basic illustration of the factor of "the move," return to the previous simple king-against-king demonstration. That is, place a White king on 4, and a Black king on 29.

Now, whoever goes first can win . . . by forcing the opposite side to retreat and finally get pinned against the side of the board. You have already seen how this works.

In such a situation, the side that holds the potential of pursuing is said to have "the move" or "the opposition."

But don't think that having "the move" necessarily guarantees a win. Take the same setup, but advance the Black king's initial position to square 22 (instead of 29). If White goes first (4 to 8), he still has the move on Black—and can still force Black to give way before him. But Black is now able to get to a Double Corner. Then White's exercise of the opposition could keep Black confined there, but Black draws by seesaw action.

"Having the move" expresses a relationship of opposition that exists at any stage. This relationship always exists with equal forces, no matter how many or how few pieces are on the board. (It is not confined only to one-against-one confrontation, as in our rudimentary example.) As a possible guiding factor, it rarely assumes any importance before the end-game. But then it *may* merit major consideration, signalling possible trouble for the pursued.

All this may not be very meaningful to you yet—but patience! The power of "the move" will be revealed with startling clarity later on in my discussion of two important end-game classics, First Position and Second Position.

14　Who's Got "The Move"?

As you enter the end-game with equal pieces, how can you tell whether or not you have "the move"?

Experienced players can discern this by inspection, but for the less experienced, the use of a simple arithmetical formula will do as well. (Use only when equal number of pieces on both sides.)

When it is your turn to play, count all checkers (regardless of color) that are in your four columns only. Your four columns proceed upward from the four playing squares of your own king row, terminating just beneath your opponent's king row. These columns contain a total of sixteen playing squares. A king counts as one, the same as an uncrowned checker.

If the total count is ODD, you have "the move."

If the total count is EVEN, your opponent has "the move." It's that simple!

Now you'll observe that there is an apparently inexorable aspect about this. For, as you can verify, no further sequence of playing moves will alter that relationship! Make any number of (nonjumping) moves alternately for both sides, and the opposition still remains the same as before. Or, as the mathematician might say, the parity structure is unaltered.

How, then, can you reverse the opposition if you desire to do so?

15 Changing "The Move"

Let us say that you are nearing the end-game phase with equal checkers, and you are trying to evaluate your position. Many elements can enter into such evaluation. Sometimes the factor of the opposition (who has "the move") may be of prime importance; experience and familiarity will tell you when having "the move" is a significant, even a vital, factor.

You count all pieces in your four columns. (In checker parlance these columns are called "your system," the remaining four columns "opponent's system.") Let us say that the total count proves to be EVEN—indicating that you do NOT have "the move."

What can you do now to reverse the opposition; that is, to alter matters so that you DO have "the move"?

The answer is this: To make a change of opposition, you must make an exchange of checkers.

I must qualify this statement. There are many kinds of exchanges. But the most common—the one you will encounter most often—is the one-for-one "transfer" exchange. In the "transfer" exchange, the piece that first jumps is the piece that is next taken. This type of exchange reverses the opposition.

Here is a simple illustration of a "transfer" exchange. Place Black on 15 and 20, place White on 28 and 32. White to play.

As an odds-evens count shows, White does *not* have "the move." (You can readily see that if White should move 32-27, Black would stop him cold with 15-19).

Fortunately, White can make the type of one-for-one exchange that transfers the opposition from one side to the other. He does so, proceeding 28-24, 20-27, 32-23—and lo! "the move" has been reversed. The "transfer" exchange did the trick!

Observe how, in this exchange, the checker that first jumped was the one next taken. (Here, the Black checker from square 20.)

Another, less frequent, kind of one-for-one exchange is the "extended" type. In this, the checker that first jumps is *not* the checker that is taken. This type of exchange does *not* reverse "the move."

Here is one example of an 'extended' exchange: Black kings on 15 and 18, White kings on 16 and 22. White to play; it can be verified that he has "the move."

White moves 16-11, and whichever jump Black takes, the resulting captures still retain "the move" for White. Note how, in this "extended" type of exchange, the piece that first jumps is *not* the piece that is next taken.

There are other kinds of exchanges of even rarer occurrence. For example, you may threaten to capture a checker on one part of the board, and your opponent retaliates by threatening to capture one of your checkers elsewhere, instead of trying to save his threatened checker. After both jumps, we have attained, in effect, a one-for-one exchange.

The effect on the opposition of such exchanges, involving rather unrelated pieces, cannot be determined through either of the two simple rules (i.e., rules for the "transfer" and the "extended" types). I *could* present the more complicated formula applicable here, but since such exchanges are less frequent, you may do as well by trying to visualize the outcome of each and then calculate "the move" at that resulting stage.

So far we have considered only the effect of one-for-one exchanges. What about the effect of multiple exchanges, such as two-for-two, three-for-three, and so on? I'll leave it to you to check these out.

Of course, the exchange you desire may not be readily available. In that case, it is up to you to plan ahead, if possible, toward creating a situation where you can force an exchange. A beautiful illustration of this appears in the delineation of Second Position, presented later.

Even if you can't initiate the desired exchange, you may find a way to force your opponent to initiate one; the reversal effect on "the move" is the same.

16 The Dog-Hole. Effect

Much of the beauty of Checkers lies in its charming inconsistencies and delightful surprises. In any given situation, all may not be what seems evident on the surface—and one must always be on the alert for the unexpected.

I have previously stated, and demonstrated, that "to make a change of opposition, you must make an exchange of checkers"—the "transfer" type of exchange.

This is true. You've got to make an exchange. You cannot reverse the opposition by simply *moving* (i.e., without any jumping).

But this is not 100 percent true! There is a unique situation in which the effective opposition can be reversed *without* making an exchange. Such a situation occurs rarely, but you should know about it so that you do not overlook the opportunity when it arises.

I shall give you a basic example of such a situation, show you how to implement it for a reversal of "the move," and then try to explain the logic of this apparent exception to the rule.

Set up this position. White on 32, king on 26. Black on 17 and 24. White to move.

Now, as a "systems" count will show, White does *not* have the opposition. Nor is there any opportunity here for White to force an exchange.

Yet, White can obtain the effective opposition by a simple maneuver, thus: White moves 26-31. Black can hold the opposition by 17-22, but, now he faces the immediate necessity of attending to White's threat to win by gaining a checker by 32-28. So, in self-protection, Black is forced instead to move 24-28. (Into the Dog Hole!)

Now the White king moves back, 31-26, then 17-21, 26-22, and behold!—the Black checker gets trapped by White having "the move" on it. White wins.

The "systems" count now will still show that *apparently* Black (not White) has "the move." Yet, obviously, White now holds the ascendency over Black—and we may properly say that White has the *effective* opposition. How come?

Well, in this unique situation, you must ignore the two opposing checkers in the Double Corner when you make the "systems" count. Try it, and you'll see that White has the opposition (as calculated before his 31-26 move).

To understand the reason for this, you must appreciate that *usually* a checker must be TWO squares away from an opposing checker in order to contain it. (You can see this in the final situation just shown; the Black man on 21 finds himself two squares away from the White king, and can only move into capture).

But, in the unusual "Dog Hole" situation shown here, the White piece on 32 effectively prevents the Black piece on 28 from moving—even though it is only ONE (not two) squares away. This situation would reverse our usual "systems" count formula, but we can restore the formula by simply pretending that these two checkers are not on the board when we make that count.

17 Two Most Important Winning Endings

Getting "the move" may put you in the driver's seat, but this does not guarantee that you have a winning position. However, when you can obtain "the move" in the end-game, you should probe deeply to discern if a winning combination does possibly exist. Because, in a great many endings with equal pieces where one side can force a win, "the move" is often a determining factor.

Among those endings where having "the move" *does* translate into a forced win, two are most notable. One of these is a two-against-two situation called "First Position." The other is a three-against-three situation called "Second Position."

These two winning situations can develop so often that it is important that you ground yourself thoroughly in the procedures required to force the wins. To the untutored player there is nothing in either situation to suggest a forced win, and almost invariably he abandons each as a draw.

So that you never do the same, I devote the pages immediately following to demonstrate how to win "First Position" and "Second Position." You cannot even *begin* to consider yourself a good checker player until you know these well. Take time out now for their special study!

18 First Position

BLACK on 12, king on 28
WHITE on 20, king on 15
White to move and win.

Set up this board situation. It represents a key stage of First Position. There are numerous other stages all of which have certain identifying characteristics in common; this aspect will be discussed in the next chapter. There you will also see how all of these evolve into some phase of the winning procedure given in *this* chapter.

In the position now before you, you have White, it is your turn to move, and you can force a win. Here the important winning factor is that White (as you can verify) has "the move." If it were Black's turn to play *he* would have "the move", and the position would be a draw.

The first step in White's winning procedure is to obtain a second king while confining the Black checker to square 12. Proceed:

15-19, 28-32, 20-16, 32-28, 16-11, 28-32, 11-7, 32-27, 7-2, 27-32, 2-7, 32-27, 7-11, 27-32, 11-15, 32-28, 15-18, 28-32, 18-23, 32-28, 23-27, 28-32, 19-23, 32-28 (12-16 loses quickly by 27-24), 27-32.

Black sees that 12-16 here loses in short order by 32-27, so he moves 28-24. White replies 23-18 (*not* 32-28, 24-19, drawn). Now the fun begins!

For, as you can verify, Black here has some options. He can avail himself of any one of four moves. But all this avails him nought! No matter which move he selects, there is no escape.

In the continuation that follows, the "Trunk Line" shows how White forces a win against Black's most stubborn defense. The "Variations" tell how White forces a win against other defensive moves that Black can choose at this, and other, critical stages. (Alphabetical letters are used for cross-references to the variations.)

Trunk Line

First master this Trunk Line. When you think you understand it thoroughly, proceed to do the same for all Variations.

Continue now after White's previous (23-18) move. As already noted, Black now has four possible choices here. Variations A, B, and C cover White's winning play against three of these. The fourth (most stubborn defense) is 24-28; this is where our Trunk Line begins. So: 24-28—A,B,C, 18-15, 28-24—F, 32-28, 24-27—G, 15-18, 12-16, 28-32, 27-24.

Then, 18-15, 24-28—H, 15-11, 16-19—J, 32-27, 28-32, 27-31, 32-28, 11-16, 19-24 (or 19-23), 16-19. White wins.

Variations

The best way to master these is to start anew before entering into a Variation. That is, review all moves from the initial (diagram) position right up to where the Variation occurs.

A—If 24-20, then 32-27, 20-16, 18-15, 16-20, 15-11, 12-16, 11-15. White wins.

B—If 12-16, then 18-15 is back into Trunk, at the start of its last paragraph.

C—If 24-19, then 32-28, 12-16—D, 28-32, 16-20—E, 32-28, 19-16 (if 20-24, 18-23 wins), 18-23, 16-11, 23-19, 11-8. Now the other White king moves in for the kill. 28-32, 8-3, 32-27, 3-8, 27-23, 8-3, 23-18, 3-7, 18-15. White wins.

D—If 19-16, then 18-15, 16-20, 15-11, 12-16, 28-32, 16-19, 11-15, 19-24 (if 20-24, 32-27 wins. Or if 19-23, 15-19, 23-26, 19-24 wins), 32-28, 24-27, 28-32, 27-31, 15-19, 31-26, 19-24. White wins.

E—If 19-24, then 18-15 is back into Trunk, at the start of its last paragraph.

F—If 12-16, then 15-11 is back into Trunk, at the third move of its last paragraph.

G—If 24-20, then 15-11 is into Variation D at its fourth move.

H—If 16-19, 32-27 wins. Or if 16-20, then 15-18, 24-28—I, 18-23 wins.

I—If 24-19, then 32-28 is into Variation C at its sixth move.

J—If 16-20, then 11-16, 28-24, 32-28, 24-27, 16-19. White wins.

42

It is important for you to realize that the kind of finesse called for in the First-Position win is not acquired by merely committing the moves to memory. You must gain insight into the reasons for the tactics employed. The habit of making reasoned evaluations is what distinguishes the expert from the ordinary player.

In our First-Position situation, White knows that because he has "the move" he may well be able to make Black toe the line. So White plans to force the Black king out of the Double Corner and yet not allow him to escape to the opposite Double Corner. Meanwhile, White keeps the Black single man under control, choosing the proper time to release him—and then being sure that this man never gets to crown in the Double Corner. Having "the move", White avoids the transfer exchange, but is ready to take any extended exchange that leaves Black off the Double-Corner Lines.

19 First Position—Precognition

The value of knowing, as you now do, that there is such a winning theme as First Position is that its emergence in a game can often be anticipated. That is to say, when certain characteristics take form, you recognize a stage of First Position. And there are numerous two-against-two situations each of which can be properly called a stage of First Position. Many of these are early stages in which neither side has yet obtained a king.

Thus you are able to predict many moves ahead that you will win, and fulfill that claim . . . to your perhaps most skeptical opponent!

In any two-against-two position where at least one of your opponent's pieces is not a king, you look for a First-Position win when all the following elements exist:

1—You have "the move", and. . . .
2—You have, or can develop, two kings while keeping an opposing single checker pinned to the right side of your board, and. . . .
3—Your opponent's other checker, although it does get a crown in your Double Corner, can be prevented from reaching the opposite Double Corner.

Here's one example of an early First Position: no kings. Place Black men on 12 and 28, White men on 7 and 20. White to move; after 7-2 (king), 28-32 (king), 2-7, 32-27, 7-10, 27-24, 10-15, 24-28, 15-19, we have First Position as depicted in the preceding chapter.

If the Black single man is on square 3 or square 4, White can compel him to advance to square 12. To illustrate, place Black man on 3, Black king on 32, and White man on 10, White king on 19. Black, we may suppose, will resist moving from square 3, but he will eventually be forced to square 12. Here's how: 10-6, 32-28 (3-7 loses by 19-15), 6-2 and king, 28-32, 2-6, 32-28, 6-10, 28-32, 10-15, 32-28, 15-18, 28-32, 18-23, 32-28, 23-27, 28-32, 19-23, 32-28 (3-7 soon loses the checker by 27-24, etc.), 27-32, 28-24 (3-7 soon loses the checker by 32-27, etc.), 32-28, 24-20, 23-19, 20-24—A, 19-15, 24-27, 15-18, 27-32—B, 18-23, 3-8, (3-7 soon loses the checker by 28-24, etc.), 28-24, 32-28, 24-19, 28-32, 19-16, 32-28, 23-19, 8-12 (forced, at last!), 16-20 into the First Position ending previously detailed.

Variations

A—If now 3-8, then 28-32, 8-12, 32-27, 20-16, 19-15, 16-20, 15-11, 12-16, 11-15. White wins.
B—If now 3-8, then 28-32, 27-24, 18-15, 24-20, 15-19, 8-12, 32-27, 20-16, 19-15, 16-20, 15-11, 12-16, 11-15. White wins.

The same procedure is used if Black's checker is on square 4 instead of square 3. But if it is on square 1 or 2, or has free access to White's left-side border, White cannot force a win.

The ability to foresee First Position has also a *defensive* value. Against an expert opponent you may be able to anticipate the danger of *your* landing into the First Position net, and avoid being so ensnared.

A good illustration of this is the following innocent-appearing position, one that may easily arise in a game.

Place Black men on 12, 13, 14, 19, and White men on 21, 22, 26, and 30. White to move. How should he proceed?

Obviously, 26-23, 19-26, 30-23, then 12-16. So far, so good. Now what?

Wouldn't you, playing White, quite naturally move 22-18? Isn't that the logical follow-up? At first blush, yes!

Blush of sheer embarrassment. That "logical" 22-18 move loses! Black obtains the winning side of First Position simply by replying 16-19. This extended exchange retains the move for him.

White's correct procedure is *not* 22-18 at this stage, but 23-19, 16-23, and *then* 22-18. After this "pitch and squeeze" maneuver the position is no more than a draw. Black can proceed 23-26, but he has lost "the move" and therefore has no First Position.

20 Second Position—See 80 Moves Ahead!

BLACK on 20, 21, king on 25.
WHITE on 30, 31, king on 28.
White to move and win.

Set up this board situation. It is a classic example of Second Position, and will serve to demonstrate the winning procedure for any phase of this end-game situation.

As with First Position, this theme occurs at various stages each identifiable as Second Position because of certain characteristics common to all. These characteristics are:

1—Three against three.

2—The winning side (here, White) has "the move."

3—White is able to pin down two Black pieces, one to square 21 and the other to an opposite border of the board.

4—Black's third man is, or can become, a king. The scope of this king is limited by White's exercise of the power of "the move."

Paradoxically, although Second Position requires many more moves to win than does First Position, the win is much easier to execute.

In fact, you can see more than eighty moves ahead once you understand how White's strategy unfolds according to the following plan:

1. Crown all your men, while keeping the two Black men pinned to the sides.

46

2. Drive the one Black king to his own Double Corner. Here, as you will see, he can be forced to yield to an exchange. This exchange will lose "the move" for White, but—
3. Then force a SECOND exchange swapping off the Black man on your right border. This will restore "the move" to White . . . with forces down to one king against one king. And, because the second exchange is properly timed, the lone Black king will be cut off from reaching a Double Corner.

With the above program in mind, as you proceed with the play that follows try to discern the reason for each move, observing how it implements the conceived strategy for the win.

31-27, 25-22, 28-24, 22-18, 24-19, 18-22—A, 19-15, 22-17, 15-18, 17-13, 18-22, 13-9, 30-26, 9-14, 26-23, 14-10, 23-18, 10-6, 18-14, 6-1, 14-9, 1-5, 9-6, 5-1, 6-2, 1-5, 2-6, 5-1, 6-10, 1-5, 10-15, 5-9, 15-19, (changing guard of square 20), 9-14, 27-23, 14-10, 23-18, 10-6, 18-14, 6-1, 14-9, 1-5, 9-6, 5-1, 6-2, 1-5, 2-6, 5-1, 6-9, 1-5, 9-14, 5-1, 14-18, 1-6, 18-23, 6-10, 23-27 (important! This second changing of guard *must* take place before making the exchange that will soon be forced), 10-14, 19-23, 14-10, 23-18, 10-6, 18-14, 6-1, 14-9, 1-5, 22-17 (We told you so!), 5-14, 17-10 (White has now lost "the move." But sweet are the uses of adversity. Watch what happens!) 21-25, 10-15, 25-30, 15-19, 30-26, 27-32 (the necessity for having previously brought this king to 27 becomes apparent), 26-22, 19-24 (now—that *second* exchange, to restore "the move" to White), 20-27, 32-23, and Black is nipped in the bud. . . 22-17, 23-18, 17-13, 18-14. White wins.

Variation A: 18-14, 27-23, 14-17, 23-18, 17-22, 18-15, 22-18, 15-11, 18-14, 11-7, 14-10, 7-2, 10-14, 2-6, 14-17, 6-9, 17-13, 9-14, 13-17, 14-18, 17-13, 18-22, 13-9, 30-26, 9-14, 26-23, 14-10, is now same as Trunk line at the 36th move.

It must be emphasized that any example given to demonstrate a winning (or drawing) theme does not represent the *only* exact layout of checkers in which that theme can be utilized. As already indicated, First Position can present itself at stages other than the one we have diagrammed. This is just as true of Second Position.

What is important is that you recognize the characteristic elements that identify the positions and make possible the effective use of the thematic ideas. Consequently, too, you must understand how the themes are properly put into force. Merely trying to learn the moves by rote is not enough.

21 The American Position

A king placed on any square of the open board always has at least two adjoining exit squares available. True?

Not true! There are two exceptions to this statement, square 4 and square 29. Each, of course, is one of the two Single-Corner squares.

A king in a Single Corner has as little, or less, mobility than has an uncrowned man anywhere on the board. That is to say, he does not have a king's usual prerogative of alternatives, but is limited to but ONE square for his next move.

The casual player is usually unaware of the special, constricting influence of the Single Corner. This unawareness costs him many a game. And conversely, it often results in his permitting a win to slip through his fingers.

The importance of this cannot be overemphasized. The different end-game situations that illustrate this stricture are too numerous to show here. However, many of these are related to the theme of the "American Position" (credited to Dr. T. J. Brown, pioneer in elucidating many important end-game themes).

So now—with the White side near you, set up the following, Dr. Brown's "American Position."

Black on 13, king on 21. White kings on 3 and 14. White to move and win!

Although White has "the move" or opposition, it hardly seems possible that he could, from this stage, make effective winning use of it. After all, he cannot prevent Black from obtaining a second king to cooperate with his other king. Two kings against two actively cooperating kings—surely this is no promise of a forced win?

Well, in this type of situation it is! White can force a win by driving Black into the constricted confines of the Single-Corner region. Here's how. 3-7, 13-17, 7-10, 17-22, 14-18 (necessary; the natural 10-15 only draws), 22-25—A, 18-22, 25-29, 22-26, 21-25, 26-30, 25-21—B, 10-14, 29-25, 14-18, 25-29, 18-22 . . . White wins.

A—If 22-26, 10-14, 21-25, 14-17, 25-21, 17-22. White wins. Or if, 21-25, 18-23, 25-21, 10-14, 22-25, 23-26, 25-29, 26-30, 29-25, 14-18, 25-29, 18-22. White wins.

B—Mark well the position here. It is at this stage that you may often encounter the American Position idea.

Even more basic to an understanding of the Single-Corner stricture is the oft-occurring ending I shall now describe. It can properly be considered a phase of the American Position.

Two against two, White to move. Place Black man on 21 and king on 29. Place White king on 26, and . . . the other White checker (which may be an uncrowned piece or a king) MAY BE PLACED ANYWHERE ELSE ON THE BOARD! Take your choice, it makes no difference—White can always win. Moreover, the forced win is there regardless of who has "the move."

How? Simply by keeping the White king posted on 26 while the other White checker obtains a crown and then moves in for the kill. The king on 26 never leaves that square until it is time to deliver the final, crushing blow.

Try it yourself. You'll see how the Black king is limited to seesawing between 29 and 25, in a futile effort to forestall the inevitable. Because, after White has brought a second king down to square 18, Black's doom becomes apparent.

22 The Bridge of Sighs

In Venice there is a bridge known as the Ponte dei Sospiri, the Bridge of Sighs. Over this bridge prisoners were taken to and from the hall of judgment.

In Checkers there is a structure which the expert may well appreciate as having some analogy to this. It is the "Bridge" position. For to the expert checker player, being compelled to enter the Bridge is usually cause for fear and trepidation.

What is a Bridge position? Well, to begin with, place a Black checker on square 1 and another Black checker on square 3. You now have formed a simple "Bridge" on the Black side.

Now, to even out the forces, let's supply White with two checkers. In doing so, we'll assume that White has a natural, and laudable, ambition to make a king. Also, for the sake of this demonstration, pretend that only White is to make any moves.

A moment's reflection will show that, in such a situation, White must proceed as follows:

1. Bring a White checker to square 10 and leave it there. (Place a White piece on 10.)
2. Escort another White checker through either of two passageways (that is, via square 6 or via square 7).

In actual practice, of course, there will be other pieces on the board . . . otherwise Black could not "stay put" this way.

The next two illustrations will deal with such a real situation, still with equality of opposing pieces. However, I shall now demonstrate that, despite even pieces, the side that maintains the Bridge (here, Black) may have an advantage.

Just so that you get the feel of it, take White—the side that can easily find itself disadvantaged because of an opposing Bridge.

Plack Black on 1, 3, and king on 13. Place White on 10, 12, and king on 2. Black to move.

Black moves 13-9, White has only 2-7, then Black goes 9-6 and White must lose his checker on 10.

Now set up the same initial position with two more checkers added, thus: Black on 1, 3, and kings on 11, 13. White on 10, 12, and kings on 2, 26.

Black moves 13-9, and on his next move he can capture the White checker on 10 by either 9-14 or 11-15.

You can now understand why there usually is an inherent disadvantage for the side that must enter the Bridge. The main vulnerability lies with the keystone piece (here the White checker on 10), which may be threatened with extinction. Apart from this, there is the limitation of movement imposed upon the defending king. He is a virtual prisoner who dares not leave the proximity of the keystone piece if he is to have any hope of protecting it.

Yes, you might well sigh when entering the Bridge, for the burden of finding a draw may rest heavily upon your shoulders. Although not every Bridge situation is indefensible, the possible drawing route may be difficult to find. In fact, one special end-game problem situation is called "Petterson's DRAW-bridge," for obvious reasons. (I'm tempted to add that Petterson's is a squeaky drawbridge escape.)

Holding your opponent in your Bridge may even have value defensively; it may gain you a draw when you are a checker down. Exactly when and how this is true depends upon the total situation.

Do not get the impression that you must avoid entering an opposing Bridge no matter what. Generally, it is better to have kinged and bridged than not to have kinged at all.

For, while an opposing Bridge may be fraught with danger, crowning through it is still advisable if there is no other readily available route. Certainly if your opponent cannot develop kings to attack your potentially vulnerable keystone checker, then your king may be free to emerge and wreak havoc on him.

However, given the choice, it is almost always wiser to break the Bridge before making a king, rather than enter the Bridge for a king.

What is meant by "breaking the Bridge"? Essentially, you break the Bridge by an exchange, as shown in the following illustration:

Black on 1, 3, king 32. White on 10, 15, 23. White to move. Instead of going for a king by 15-11, the procedure as recommended is 23-19, to be followed up by 10-6 . . . breaking the Bridge.

Moreover, even if you already find yourself with a king inside the Bridge, it may be wise to plan to break that Bridge later. A line-up of checkers for an exchange, as in the example just shown, is the usual procedure. Or, sometimes, you can move your keystone checker forward to sacrifice it provided your king can then be sure of recapturing safely.

The Bridge dealt with here is formed by checkers on 1 and 3. (Or, correspondingly for White, on 32 and 30.) As you have seen, this Bridge can be a potent device. Now, another Bridge sometimes occurs, formed by checkers on 2 and 4 (or, for White, on 31 and 29). While this too may have a certain effectiveness, it generally proves inferior to the other Bridge.

From all the foregoing you might easily be led to conclude that one should hold on to his two Bridge squares relentlessly, never moving from 1 and 3 (or, for White, from 32 and 30), throughout the entire game.

Reasonable as this may seem, it would be bad advice. For, any self-imposed restriction that reduces your mobility as compared to your opponent's can be injurious. The immediate consequence of the board situation is what you must *first* consider at each stage, even though you may keep some eye toward the eventual end-game. And the immediate situation may demand that you move a Bridge checker.

Checkers has many of such paradoxes. That is why you will often find here warnings of conditional exceptions after statements of advice. ("It is good to keep your Bridge—but not if it otherwise hurts your position.")

The examples of Bridge Position situations that I have used for illustration represent very elementary aspects. For a true appreciation of the depth and beauty in Bridge Positions, I recommend the book *Bridges in the Game of Checkers* by Ben Boland.

Ben Boland is the indefatigable scribe whose lifetime avocation is to compile end-game themes for the edification and delight of the serious Checker enthusiast. To this end he has written and published many books. Boland's *Bridges* contains 234 diagrams, each representing a different Bridge Position situation. Each, of course, is accompanied by copious analyses and explanatory notes.

23 Center and Side Remarks

Generally speaking, a checker in the center is to be preferred to one at the side. A side checker usually has less potential mobility, and furthermore there is often the danger that it may stay pinned there and thus incur a weakness in the end-game. So, everything else being equal, prefer a move to the center to one to the side.

Since, however, everything else is not always equal, this generality needs to be taken with a grain of salt. For one thing, moving White into the side square 13, or correspondingly, Black into 20, has a certain compensatory effectiveness in that it poses some threatening influence on the opposing Double Corner—similar to, though not as potently, as does solid control of the Dyke square (14 or 19).

There are many other instances in which a move to the side is effectively indicated. Sometimes, the intent of such a move is to preclude the threat of capture. And in certain positions, the effect of a side move is to cramp some of the opposing pieces, thereby limiting their choice of good moves.

A typical example of the latter may be noted in Black's handling of the Switcher opening. (While White can draw after getting into the Switcher formation, the burden of proof falls upon him.) The Switcher begins thus, 11-15, 21-17. Now, of all the possible replies at Black's command the best is the side move, 9-13. Why? Because with that one move Black has placed into a cramp the four White pieces on 17, 22, 25 and 29. In fact, before White can attend to other aspects of his game, he must concentrate on relieving that cramp. Otherwise he can lose through eventual loss of mobility.

Typically, White's next step would be to move 25-21, thereby aiming to occupy 14 next, through an exchange. Black's best reply now is to allow this (you'll soon see why), and so he goes 8-11. Now White may elect to wait with 30-25 before making the exchange, but this 30-25 does create a subtle (though defensible) weakness. Or he may make the 17-14 exchange immediately, the more characteristic reply. This gives White the Dyke square, but Black's next move, 6-10, forces 22-17 (29-25 eventually loses). Then, after 13-22, 26-17, White's occupancy of the Dyke square becomes jittery. His pieces on 14 and 17 have no mobility and must ever be carefully guarded against attack.

This is a kind of position the beginner must learn to recognize as requiring a side move for effective control. An analogous position occurs when Black begins with the Dundee opening, 12-16. White's best reply follows the same principle; by now moving 24-20 he places Black under (at least temporary) constraint.

Apart from all this, there is a large class of checker formations in which one side encourages the other to take the center, meanwhile surrounding his pieces with the threat of getting them all clogged up—impeding each other's mobility. Then what few moves remain available to the aggressor may all be bad ones. Recognition of such situations comes only with experience, foresight and examination of published play. Such recognition is required for *both* sides; the side that seeks domination of the center too must look ahead—to anticipate where he should change his tactics to avoid being caught in a bind.

Here is one example of what I mean; it is the type of loss the beginner may easily drift into, to his bewildered dismay. In this game Black drives a powerful wedge into White's center, incautiously oblivious of the fact that White, in constantly opening the way, has no meek intent. Observe: 11-15, 23-19, 8-11, 22-17, 4-8, 25-22, 9-14, 29-25, 5-9, 17-13, 14-18, 26-23, 9-14, 22-17, 1-5, 30-26, 5-9, 26-22—and Black is lost. (What profiteth it him to gain the center if he loseth the game?)

Where, you may ask, did Black go wrong? Well, at his fourth move (9-14) he would have been wiser to move 9-13 instead. By switching to a side move, which here tends to cramp White, Black maintains his attack while avoiding the danger of overextending his ambitious drive.

24 Shots, Strokes, and Such

Catch a player by the shot,
Jump his checkers, grab the lot.
If he hollers, let him bawl;
That's the way to win them all!
                              —Heywood Pusher

How often do we see such a harum-scarum portrait of Checkers on television and movie screen! Two players are locked in crossboard combat. One of them meekly offers a checker for capture, this is greedily gobbled up by his gloating opponent. Then—slam, bang!—the first player jumps all over the board removing every one of his opponent's pieces.

Is this what the game of Checkers is all about? Is winning just a matter of luring your opponent into a shot (three for one, or whatever) and then mopping up the board?

Not really. Despite its pyrotechnic appeal, the spectacular shot is not what you should strive for in your games. Of course if your opponent generously presents you with a winning shot, you will take it. But in shaping up the course of your own game, your constant aim should be towards achieving positional superiority, *not* towards tricking your opponent into a shot trap.

The material in this book will guide you towards an understanding of what constitutes positional superiority. Study of high-level games as played between masters will re-enforce that understanding.

The slam-bang view of Checkers is simplistic and trivializing. The game is far more subtle than that. As with "the sweet science" of boxing, there's more to scientific Checkers than tearing in and swinging roundly in the hope of obtaining a quick knockout. Dreams of glory in which you zing some checker expert with a killer-diller shot—are rarely realized. Among the really top-caliber players a win never* occurs as a result of one player falling for a shot. Because, both players are presumed to be equally capable of foreseeing the shot.

Having apparently minimized the importance of shots, I now present you with a Checker paradox. To become an expert checker player you *must*, among other things, develop the ability to visualize all sorts of shots, from the simplest to the very complicated. (The latter are also known as "strokes.")

If you can't see shots, you'll lose games by falling into them, and you'll fail to take winning shots that may be there. In either case, the shot need not have been set up deliberately; shot potentialities constantly occur in the normal course of positional play.

But there is something more basic strategically, and that is the key point of this discussion. In high-class scientific Checkers (which is your goal), although a winning shot rarely takes place, the shots are always there . . . but lurking in the shadows! For it is the *threat* of a shot that is the behind-the-scenes operator. This is how and why:

In reply to a positional formation that embodies the *threat* of a winning shot, a discerning player must seek a move that avoids the shot. Occasions arise where such a threat may be used to force an opponent into a line of play desired by the forcing player, possibly a weak or losing continuation. The shot, so to speak, operates by remote control to make the opponent toe the line.

For one illustration of this, place Black on 16, 18, 28, and White on 24, 32, king on 13. White to move and win.

White moves 13-17, threatening a two-for-one shot if Black replies 16-20, which *would* draw if there were no shot. Black, seeing this threat, is forced to his only other choice, 18-23. White then replies 17-22, then 16-20, 32-27!, 23-32, 22-26, 20-27, 26-31 . . . and Black, unable to move, loses. White's *threat* of a shot forced Black into this sad predicament.

The ability to visualize shots develops with experience and study, especially of problems. You learn to look for "holes" in your opponent's structure that may portend the possibility of a shot, and also to look for ways to produce such "holes." Similarly, you learn to guard against shot vulnerability on your side.

The number and variety of shots that are possible on the checkerboard are enormous. The 30 positions that follow illustrate some of the more important basic shot themes. Have fun!

---

*What, never? Well, hardly ever. The occasions when a Checker master has stumbled into an avoidable shot are few and far between, and usually attributable to inadvertence, exhaustion, or the "blind staggers."

25 Can You Spot the Shot?

Each of the 30 positions given below depends upon a shot idea for its solution. As problems they range from the very easy to the difficult. However, they are not presented to test your ability, but to give you practice towards improving your powers of visualization.

Set up and tackle each in turn. Spot the shot, and you've solved the problem. For any that elude you, refer to the Solution Clues that follow.

Remember, the terms for each problem are WHITE TO MOVE AND WIN. Also bear in mind that even if it doesn't immediately gain a checker, it's still considered a shot if after all the jumps are made you've gained a win.

Abbreviations used are: B for Black, W for White, k for king.

1—B 9, 17, 19. W 27, 31.
2—B 11, 18, 19. W 26, 31.
3—B 10, 18, 20. W 27, 32.
4—B 13, 18, 20. W 24, k27.
5—B 9, 11, 20. W 18, 28, 32.
6—B 10, 12, 26. W 19, 23, 30.
7—B 5, 9, 11, 20. W 18, 23, 28, 32.
8—B 9, 12, 17. W 19, 26, 31.
9—B 9, 10, 19. W 18, 27, 31.
10—B 5, 14, 18, 20. W 21, 28, 29, 32.
11—B 10, 11, 17. W 19, 26, 30.
12—B 7, 11, 17, 19. W 18, 26, 28, 30.
13—B 5, 10, 12, 17. W 18, 20, 23, 31.
14—B 13, 14, 19. W 25, 27, 31.
15—B 2, k25, k26. W 10, 19, k14.

16—B 3, k26, k27. W 11, 16, k19.
17—B 3, 5, 19, k18. W 10, 14, k13.
18—B 2, 5, k18, k26. W 9, 14, k8.
19—B 5, 13, k11, k23. W 14, 22, k10.
20—B 5, 11, 13, k23. W 14, 17, 22, k10.
21—B k14, k24. W k10, k17, k23.
22—B 5, k15, k23. W 6, 9, 14.
23—B 8, 11, 15, 18, 23. W 20, 22, 25, 27, 32.
24—B 2, 5, k22, k24. W 9, 14, 23, k1.
25—B 1, 6, 9, k25. W 13, 15, 22, k2.
26—B 3, 6, 8, 13. W 14, 17, 22, 30.
27—B 5, 9, 20, k25. W 23, 26, 28, 32.
28—B 7, 15, 20, 24. W 27, 29, 30, 31.
29—B 9, 13, 17, 25, k29. W 18, 22, 26, k32.
30—B 9, 10, 11, 20, k17. W 23, 24, 26, k27.

Solution Clues

Only the first White move is given for each, the rest is more or less obvious.

(1) 27-23. (2) 26-23. (3) 27-24. (4) 27-32. (5) 18-15. (6) 19-15. (7) 28-24. (8) 19-16. (9) 18-14. (10) 21-17. (11) 19-15. (12) 26-22. (13) 18-15. (14) 25-21. (15) 10-7. (16) 11-8. (17) 10-7. (18) 14-10. (19) 22-17. (20) 22-18. (21) 23-19. (22) 14-10. (23) 20-16. (24) 14-10. (25) 15-10. (26) 22-18. (27) 28-24. (28) 31-26. (29) 26-23. (30) 27-32.

26 Tips and Hints to Improve Your Game

In the preceding chapters I have dealt mainly with certain basic themes and ideas. Knowledge of these is important; you will see how they may exert their influence in many of the solutions to the one hundred problems that follow later. These solutions, in turn, go on to reveal a great many *more* thematic ideas which you can then proceed to incorporate into your repertoire.

However, no one volume will contain all of the different themes and concepts that can develop on the board. That is one of the fascinating aspects of the game of Checkers—because its depths are fathomless, its value as a lifetime hobby is unsurpassed. Those who pursue it as such find that their interest never palls.

Having covered those certain important fundamentals, I feel I should continue with some bits of advice of a more general nature. While these are intended primarily for the beginner, the experienced player may find value in reviewing them.

1. Don't give away a checker unless your examination of the situation convinces you that the loss of a man is compensated for by an equal or better position in relation to your opponent's. Remember also to watch out for shots; falling into a two for one is the same as giving away a checker.

However, if you find yourself in a losing position, *do* consider the possibility that some timely, well-conceived sacrifice can so complicate your opponent's task as to make it more likely that he misses the winning continuation.

2. Look before you—threaten to—leap! Before you move so as to threaten a jump . . . stop, look, and consider. Ask yourself, "Is there any reply my opponent can make that will meanwhile take advantage of my being *forced* to jump?"

3. Contrariwise, whenever your opponent threatens a jump, don't automatically cover up or run away. Stop, look, and consider. Can you make use here of another move—a waiting move—to your advantage?

The importance of heeding both of these "Stop—Look—Consider" precautions is neatly illustrated in the following position. The idea is from a recent game between that esteemed old Checker patron, Carlyle Rowntree, and the writer, Jules Leopold.

Black is on 16, 17, 19, 20, king on 25. White is on 15, 23, 26, 28, king on 14. Black's turn to move.

Of course 17-22 draws. But the natural but incautious 25-22 squeeze loses! Here's how:

25-22, 14-21, 22-31. Now, if White (equally impulsive) yields to immediate protective instinct and moves away by 23-18, the game is simply a draw. Instead, a moment's pause and reflection here will lead White to proceed 21-25, 19-26, 25-30, winning!

4. Get your king into action at the earliest advisable opportunity. Don't let him languish idly. Remember, he has the power to harass the opposition. He may be able to capture uncrowned checkers, force pieces into cramped or otherwise untenable positions, hold men to the sides to produce any of numerous winning end-game situations . . . and so on.

5. Don't set up "sucker" traps if, by doing so, you weaken the integrity of your position. Respect your opponent. He may be well aware of your evil designs, avoid them, and then clobber you for your impertinence.

Instead, concentrate on maintaining a sound and viable structure. Your opponent then will have plenty of opportunities to go wrong.

The old master's advice of "Keep the draw in sight" was not intended to be a purely passive approach to the game. It was just a pithy way of saying, "Make sure you have at least a draw, before you start looking for a way to win."

6. On the other hand, if your opponent seems suddenly to have left himself wide open, don't rush in for the kill. Stop, look, and consider. Has he baited a tempting trap for you?

Move in haste and get pent up later! Always take your time, Checkers is not a test of speed. No matter how good a move looks, don't rush to make it without carefully considering consequences. Even if you then decide that it is splendid, look again. There may yet be an even better move!

7. Apart from other possible immediate considerations, it is generally a good idea to make your opponent toe the line by your selecting such moves as will minimize his choice of valid replies.

8. One way to increase the potential number of options available to you is to provide for the possibility of later moving ahead into capture without losing a checker. In other words, the added option of being able to progress via an exchange . . . rather than being limited only to ordinary moves.

This, especially in the earlier stages of a game, requires that you line up your pieces, one behind the other in support, closing up "holes."

9. Nevertheless, it is impossible to avoid the occurrence of holes in your formation as the game progresses. Before creating a hole, stop, look, and consider. Be sure that you will not thereby create an opportunity for your opponent to take a "shot" or "stroke"—like a two for one or worse.

Contrariwise, when your opponent's position shows holes, look for the same possibility for yourself.

10. Such dictums as "Don't weaken your Double-Corner region" are not to be taken unconditionally. As in Chess, the Zugzwang situation will occur; this is when you must move but would rather "stand pat" because any move creates some positional weakness.

Know then that, as the game progresses, each side may inevitably develop weak spots. No matter,—if such weaknesses tend to offset each other. Keep this in mind. The weakening of (say) your Double Corner through necessity at some stage may no longer be a *comparative* weakness after your opponent has had to yield to similar or other necessities. And, if you can't wholly defend your weakness, counterattack his weakness.

11. A stubborn refusal to move out of your king row can prove costly. Mobility is a vital resource in Checkers. You deprive yourself of some mobility if you determine not to move out of certain square no matter what. A strong king row is but one of many positional considerations that may be respected; others will often merit priority.

12. Broadly viewed, Checkers involves the judicious employment of two contradictory devices: mass and mobility. You must be ever alert as to when a shift from one to another is required. This is why:

In many openings, one side proceeds to form a compact phalanx hoping to batter down the other's defenses by sheer mass. Instead of meeting force with force, the defending side may strive to surround by a pincers movement, aiming to choke off the attacker's progress.

Confronted by signs of such defensive tactics, you must try to anticipate the stage at which your massive juggernaut could possibly be brought to a standstill. You must avoid the closing of those pincers, else you may find that your checkers have been rendered immobile. That offensive vehicle can easily become a useless, locked-in hulk.

What you must prepare for is the ability to break out, if enclosure is threatened, before it is too late. Usually a break-out is achieved by making one or more exchanges. Usually, too, your position will change in character, being one now marked by openness, fluidity and mobility. Subtler skirmishes come into play. The massing is gone but the menacing lingers on!

13. When you are clearly a checker ahead, you most likely have a forced win in hand. Finish off expeditiously; don't fool around.

Quite often this simply means that you should "swap off" the checkers, making sure that no exchange leaves your position vulnerable. Your opponent, if he hadn't gotten the message earlier, should surely resign when the count shows two checkers against his one.

Contrary to tenderhearted belief, there is nothing cruel or unsportsmanlike in this tactic. Exchanging when you are ahead is often the *only* way to consummate the win.

14. The end-game is that stage of the game where only a few pieces remain, in more or less uneasy confrontation. Having safely reached this stage, don't yield to the temptation to relax attention.

Eternal vigilance may save the day. Or bring home the bacon. Depends upon whose ox is being gored. I know I've mixed metaphors here, but that's only in a humble effort to highlight the two aspects; OFFENSIVE and DEFENSIVE, of the following things for which you should now watch out:

—Getting the first free king.
—Pinning one or more pieces to the side.
—Stealing an unprotected checker.
—Gaining a piece, or a winning position, by a "shot."
—Who has "the move", and does it matter here?
—Can one side be run out of moves?

These are some of the things to which you should remain alert at the end-game. Each should be viewed from two standpoints: what can you do to your opponent's position, and what can he do to yours—offensively and defensively.

15. Withal, seek out opponents whose game is superior to yours. Let such be your "school of hard knocks," there are few better ways to improve your crossboard ability.

But whether you play a weaker or a stronger opponent,—win or lose—be gracious. There may be some who can tolerate a sore loser, but nobody loveth a sore winner! You know—the abrasive kind who likes to rub it in when he's ahead.

27 Just for Openers

Every published problem position originated in one of two sources. Either it had arisen in an actual game, or it had sprung full-blown from the brain of a problem creator (though often after long inner struggle!).

Often, of course, the two may merge. A problemist's creation may be found to recur in a game, or vice versa. And very often an actual game situation may suggest to the problemist an idea from which he will create an original problem.

Accordingly, the problems that follow here have been arranged in two groups; (1) mostly pure compositions, and, (2) actual game-situation occurrences. The latter group also includes the run-up of moves in each game up to the problem stage.

As you follow the play in each game on your board you will become aware that different opening moves are employed in different games. They do not all start the same way.

This may strike you as odd—and inconsistent—IF you are aware that the usual expert advice on how to start is:

"Open with 11-15. This employs a piece from your Single-Corner Line to control the center. It is the strongest opening move for Black."

Such expert advice often continues with suggestions for the best White reply to 11-15. Usually this is 23-19, or 22-18; or sometimes 23-18.

Understandably then you might ask, "Why have the expert games in this book apparently ignored this advice? Certainly the experts must believe in the validity of their advice, so why do they deviate from it?"

Well, you are entitled to an explanation, and here it is.

It is true that opening your game with the "Old Faithful" 11-15 move gives you a theoretical edge, though by no means a winning one, for Checkers is a *fair* game. In game theory, a fair game is defined as one that confers no winning advantage to going first (or second, for that matter). Such a game is so evenly balanced to begin with that is must always end in a draw IF (and a mighty big IF it is!) both players play flawlessly.

The fact is that Black may open with any one of his seven possible options, and be assured that he has not yet made a losing move. He has, so to speak, the draw in hand.

However, some openers are rated as weaker than others because they are more subject to harassment by optimum aggressive counterplay. In descending order of merit, Black's seven possible opening moves are: 11-15, 9-14, 11-16, 10-15, 12-16, 10-14, and 9-13. You may guide yourself accordingly, but remember—you can gain fun and crossboard experience by defending a weaker opening, especially when nothing much is at stake.

In a general sense, 22-18 will serve adequately as White's reply to any Black opener. Better, however, to counter 10-15 with 21-17, and 12-16 with 24-20.

In the early days of Checkers, all matches and tournaments were on a "go as you please" basis, meaning that each player could start off with any available move of his choice. Usually, though not always, this resulted in Black's opening with the Old Faithful 11-15 move.

Later, as Restricted Styles (explained further on) were introduced, this "go as you please" approach was termed "Free Style" or "Unrestricted Play." (Since 1951, the world championship at this style of Checkers had been held by Tom Wiswell—until he voluntarily retired his title recently.)

What are the Restricted Styles of play, and why were they introduced? I will answer the second part of this question first.

It became apparent that the experts were able to reduce the demands upon their cerebral processes, by sticking to their pet openings (such as 11-15, 23-19). While this did not preclude an inexhaustible field for follow-up play, it did nevertheless tend somewhat toward the stereotype, especially in matches where neither opponent would venture to complicate the board situation.

So it came to pass that, to jog these experts out of their blithe complacency, a remedy was introduced in the form of the "Two-Move Restriction" ballot.

As you may readily determine, there are 7 times 7, or 49 possible combinations of the first two moves. This reduces to 47 when we eliminate the two obviously untenable ones: 9-14, 21-17 and 10-14, 21-17. (Each loses a piece for White.) We may also eliminate certain other two-movers from consideration, these being four whose defensibility for White might be regarded as dubious. This reduces the number of two-move opening possibilities to 43.

Imagine now a special deck of 43 cards, each imprinted with a different two-move opening. Before play begins, a card is drawn at random. That card dictates the first two opening moves. If, for example, the card reads "10-15,

21-17," then Black *must* open with 10-15 and White *must* reply with 21-17.

In scrupulous fairness, a pair of games are played under the selected opening, the two players reversing Black and White roles at the second game. Thereafter, another card is drawn for the next pair of games, and so on.

Such is the "Two-Move Restriction."

Before the ink had dried on the innovative two-move cards, some inspired Checkerist came forth with the suggestion of *Three*-Move Restriction.

This style of play, in which the first three moves are dictated by ballot, prevails among the top experts today. They must now be prepared to handle the limitless combinations that can arise from any of the 142 possible valid three-move openings! Here also, the two players change sides at the second of each pair of games. They also alternate as to who first plays Black at the start of each pair of games.

Now you will understand why the games recorded in this book commence from a variety of openings, despite the traditional recommendation of 11-15 perhaps followed by 23-19. Most of these games have been played by experts reared in the tradition, and compulsion, of Three-Move Restriction. Which, you may be assured, makes one a mighty sharp crossboard player at any style of play.

Just to complete the picture, I must report that still another form of restriction occasionally appears in top-level competition. It is known as Eleven-Man Ballot. Here one checker, determined randomly by ballot, is *removed* from each side prior to play—and then (usually) a two-move restriction is further imposed. This hypermodern style of play permits of a mind-boggling variety of different possible opening formations.

So there you have it! You pays your money and you takes your choice!

28 Fifty Selected Problems

Fifty tantalizing problem beauties are shown in this section. Some are pure compositions, idealized images, each sketched from its creator's imagination. Some have been suggested by analogous visions occurring in crossboard games. And some have reared their pretty heads during play; these are depicted here exactly as seen.

In the last case, complete recognition may not have been reached until later, when diligent postgame analysis revealed their hidden virtues. Yes, even the greatest of masters have been known to miss the correct solution during a game—failing to discern the proper (usually subtle but sometimes obvious) procedure. So, these studies are for all . . . novice, expert, or master. Each idea revealed can prove of value for there is no telling when recognition of its appearance may later stand you in good stead.

For those who may not have had previous acquaintance with checker problems, a few words of introduction may be in order.

A checker problem sets up a positional situation on the board and states the terms for solving it. Typically the terms tell (1) whose turn it is to move, and (2) what result must, and can, be achieved.

Examples of such terms are: White to play and win; White to play and draw; Black to play and win; Black to play and draw.

Once in a while a problem will appear whose terms require one side to move and the other side to effect the result—as, for example, "Black to move and White to draw." And sometimes a quixotic composer will present a double perplexity with such terms as "White to move and what result?" However, in all problems, the important thing to realize is that BEST PLAY ON BOTH SIDES IS ALWAYS TO BE ASSUMED, AND IT IS THE SOLVER'S TASK TO DETERMINE WHAT THAT IS. To demonstrate a WIN for your side, you must be able to show what are your opponent's best defensive moves . . . and how your countermoves will defeat them. Similarly, to demonstrate a DRAW for your side, you must deal with your opponent's best offensive plan.

Moreover, since the problems here are not intended to be trivial ones, do not dismiss any as such. If the terms are, for example, "White to move and draw," and your initial reaction is "Why should White have any problem here?" chances are that you haven't probed for Black's strongest attack. Before jumping to facile conclusions ask yourself, "What has the other side got up its sleeve?" Often the other side's attempted countermeasures are as subtle and cleverly concealed as are the solving moves of the protagonist. You cannot truly envision the correct solution if you fail to take all this into account.

All this may seem like a tough order, but, as Gertrude Stein once said, "Familiarity breeds . . . more familiarity." The more you get to know and absorb of the key ideas revealed in these pages, the more intimately familiar they will become. In time you may find that they've become, like old friends, recognizable on sight.

Of course, solutions are given. But you should first try to tackle each problem without looking at the nearby solution. And even when the problem fails to yield, don't peek yet, but return to it later. You may be surprised at how often the key idea may flash upon you after a second or third try.

Now if you see a likely-looking move that is not shown in the printed solution, probe carefully its ramifications before you conclude that it upsets the terms of the problem. You may be fairly sure that something is nix with that move. Also, you may experience a certain delight in finding out for yourself why it won't work. However, if you finally remain convinced that you *have* corrected the terms of the problem (or found an alternate solution), write us in care of the publisher. Should your correction prove valid, you'll receive credit with any future publication of the problem as corrected.

The Candidate

BLACK

WHITE

Problem No. 1
By Jack Birnman
BLACK: 24, kings 4, 8, 19, 31
WHITE: 32, kings 7, 10, 13, 28
White to play and win

Solution

7-3—A, 8-11, 10-14, 11-16—B, 32-27, 16-20, 13-9!, 31-26, 27-23, 20-16—C, 14-18, 24-27, 18-22, 26-17, 9-13, 19-26, 13-24—D. White wins.
A—Which piece is the least likely candidate to take the man on square 24? Watch the drama unfold.
B—If 31-26, 14-18, 26-30, 13-9, 30-25, 9-6, 25-21, 6-2, 21-17, 3-8, 11-16, 8-11, White wins.
C—If 24-27, 23-16, 20-11, 3-8, White wins.
D—Jack Birnman is an expert player and problemist who is also an expert on "Spanish Pool" Checkers.

The Master of Checkers and Chess

The late Newell W. Banks, one of the all-time Checker greats, once defeated both Frank Marshall and Isaac Kashdan in the same masters' Chess tournament. However, Marshall was by then well past his prime, and Kashdan was still comparatively young and inexperienced. This event later evoked the wry comment that Banks beat Marshall after Marshall was Marshall, and beat Kashdan before Kashdan was Kashdan. (No one thought to ask if Banks was really himself that day!)

Brown's Bramble Bush

BLACK

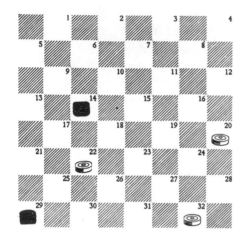

Problem No. 2
By Dr. T. J. Brown
BLACK: Kings 14, 29
WHITE: 20, 22, 32
White to play and draw

WHITE

Solution

20-16—A, 29-25, 22-17, 14-21, 16-11—B, 21-17, 32-28—C, 17-14—D, 28-24, 14-10, 24-19, 25-22, 19-16, 22-18, 11-8, 18-15, 8-3, 10-6, 3-8, 6-2, 16-11—E. Drawn.

A—Although White is a man ahead, the two Black kings threaten to engulf White if he does not play with care.

B—Nicely forcing Black's next move.

C—The key to White's salvation. The play from here on is very instructive as White avoids all the pitfalls.

D—If 25-22, 11-7, 17-14, 28-24, 22-18, 24-19, 18-23, 19-15. Drawn.

E—By the late Dr. T. J. Brown, who virtually exhausted the two-by-two problem field, while occasionally entering the three-by-two and three-by-three category. Many of his fine end-game positions appear in W. T. Call's little gem of a problem book, *Midget Problems*.

Luck and Skill

You may get a lucky break in a game, but you won't know what to do with it if you haven't developed the proper skill. Don't depend on luck in Checkers; it is a game of skill. (T.W.)

Divide and Survive

BLACK

WHITE

Problem No. 3
By Dr. T. J. Brown
BLACK: 7, kings 4, 5, 29
WHITE: kings 6, 14, 17
White to play and draw

Solution

6-2—A, 7-11, 2-7, 11-16, 7-11, 16-20, 17-22, 20-24, 14-10—B, 5-9, 10-15, 9-14, 15-19, 24-28, 19-24, 28-32, 24-28—C. Drawn.

A—Although White is a man down he has an unusual plan for securing a draw.

B—Note how White is isolating the Black forces, therein lies his strategy for survival. Now if 24-28 (instead of 5-9), 10-6 draws.

C—The Black kings cannot join forces and so the position must be called a deadlock.

Those Innocent Times!

Evangeline brought the draughts board out of its corner, soon was the game begun. In friendly contention the two men laughed at each lucky hit, or unsuccessful maneuver; laughed when a man was crowned, or a breach made in the king row. (Henry Wadsworth Longfellow)

Welsh Terrier

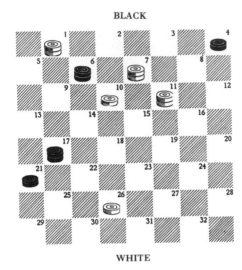

BLACK

WHITE

Problem No. 4
By J. Charles
BLACK: 4, 21, kings 6, 17
WHITE: 10, 26, kings 1, 7, 11
White to play and win

Solution

11-15—A, 6-2, 7-3—B, 2-7, 10-6, 7-2, 26-22!—C, 17-26, 3-8, 4-18, 1-5, 2-9, 5-30—D. White wins.

A—The first of a series of forcing moves that lead to a pleasing and surprising finish.

B—Of course 7-11 allows 17-14 . . . and the win disappears.

C—A typical "Charles" maneuver, the imprint of a master.

D—By the famous Welsh composer J. M. Charles. Along with Graham Davies, the 1972 British champion, Mr. Charles has kept the Draughts spotlight on his beautiful little country.

The Phantom Fox Den

The Phantom Fox Den is the name given by Bert Titus to a position that arose between Banks and Jordan in 1917. Banks won with the White side. Three years later Bert Titus, calling the position "the most deceptive thing on the checkerboard," offered to wager that he could prove it a draw "requiring of Black more than 25 consecutive star moves." He was proved wrong, but it took over a year before the analysts could demonstrate a White win against the best of Titus's subtle defenses.

The position: Black on 1, 3, 7, 10, 11, 14, 20. White on 12, 21, 22, 23, 26, 31, 32. White to move.

31-26 is the star move that leads to a White win. 'Tain't easy, though!

Phantom King

BLACK

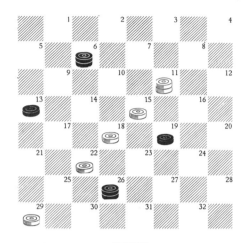

WHITE

Problem No. 5
By J. Charles
BLACK: 13, 19, kings 6, 26
WHITE: 15, 18, 22, 29, king 11
White to play and win

Solution

11-16—A, 26-17, 16-23, 6-9, 15-10—B, 17-22, 18-15, 9-14, 29-25—C, 22-29, 23-26, 14-7, 26-22, etc. White wins.

A—The start of another fine production by the great Welsh composer.

B—If 15-11, 17-22, 18-15, 9-14, 23-19, 22-18, 19-16, 14-9, 29-25, 13-17, 25-21, 17-22, 16-12, 9-14, 12-8, 22-26, etc., draws. Or, if 29-25, 17-21, 25-22, 21-17, 23-26, 17-14, draws.

C—A beautiful climax that leads to a theme utilized as far back as 1858 by the noted R. Petterson now best remembered for "Petterson's Drawbridge."

What Could Be Fairer?

If your opponent insists on a wager, you might try the cure prescribed in Jules Leopold's book of puzzles, *Check Your Wits*. Set up the following position:

Black on 19 and 21. White on 29, 30, 31. Offer to bet him (a small beer) that, moving first with Black, he won't succeed in crowning his man on 19. You'll win, because most likely he'll go 19-24, then follows 29-25, 24-28, 30-26, 21-30, 31-27, 30-32!

Now that he's seen how it's done, offer (in a burst of fairness and generosity) to take the other side of the same bet. You'll win again—because you'll first move 21-25, and then . . .!

Elementary, Dr. Watson

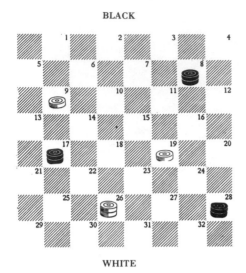

BLACK

WHITE

Problem No. 6
By J. Churchill
BLACK: kings 8, 17, 28
WHITE: 9, 19, king 26
White to play and draw

Solution

19-16—A, 8-12—B, 16-11, 17-14—B, 9-6, 14-10—B, 6-2!—C, 28-24—D,
26-22, 24-19—D, 22-17—E, 19-15, 11-8!, 3-12—F. Drawn.
A—If 26-23, 17-14, 9-6 (9-5, 28-24, 19-15, 8-12), 14-10, 6-2, 28-24,
19-16, 8-12, 16-11, 24-19, 23-16, 12-19. Black wins.
B—These are the best attacking moves for Black.
C—A fine move that saves the game for White. Watch closely.
D—Black wants to steal that man on square 11.
E—The right king on the right square at the right time!
F—A fine end-game study by the late English problemist and player.

The Black Doctor

This is an opening, 11-15, 23-19, 8-11, 22-17, 9-13, 17-14, 10-17, 19-10,
7-14, in which White gives up a checker.

The White Doctor is an opening, 11-16, 22-18, 10-14, 25-22, 8-11, 24-20,
16-19, 23-16, 14-23, 26-19 in which Black gives up a checker. In each case,
while the prognosis is a Draw, heroic treatment is prescribed for the
patient—the player who is a piece short. (J.L.)

72

Greensword's Gem

BLACK

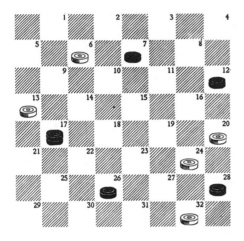

WHITE

Problem No. 7
By C. J. Greensword
BLACK: 7, 12, 26, 28, king 17
WHITE: 6, 13, 20, 24, 32
White to play and win

Solution

6-2—A, 7-11, 24-19—A, 17-14, 2-7—A, 14-18—B, 7-16, 18-23—B.
13-9—C, 26-31, 9-6—C, 31-27, 6-2—C, 27-24—D, 2-7, 24-15, 7-11!—E,
15-8, 16-19, 23-16, 20-4—F. White wins.

A—White has a beautiful combination in mind, as these forceful moves
shortly illustrate.

B—These moves constitute Black's best defense.

C—The author shows the master's touch with this perfect timing.

D—If 27-31, 2-7, 31-26, 16-11, 23-16, 7-3 or 11-15. White wins.

E—The winning theme that was envisioned as far back as Note A.

F—Mr. Greensword was a star of yesteryear and many of his gems may be
found in publications early in the twentieth century.

First Known

The first known work on modern Draughts (Checkers) was written by Anton
Torquemada and published at Valencia, Spain, in 1547. Subsequently,
Canalejas published a work on Draughts which had two editions; the second
edition contains the imprimatur of the Vicar-General of Zaragossa.

Cornucopia

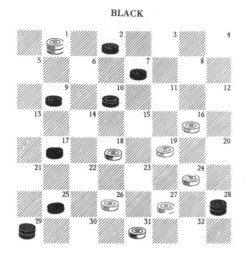

BLACK

WHITE

Problem No. 8
By A. C. Hews
BLACK: 2, 7, 9, 10, 17, 25, kings 28, 29
WHITE: 16, 18, 19, 24, 26, 27, 31, king 1
White to play and win

Solution

18-14—A, 9-18, 27-23—A, 18-27, 16-11!, 7-30, 1-5—B, 28-19, 31-6, 2-9, 5-21—C. White wins.

A—In stroke problems you must give away your men in such a way as to set up your opponent for the final coup.

B—Now White is about to reap compound interest on his shrewd investment.

C—By "Mr. Stroke Problem" himself, A. C. Hews, late of Cardiff. He was the author of *Hews' Stroke Problems*, devoted solely to his own compositions in this field—which he so long dominated.

Unplumbed Depths

Checkers or Chess—it is hard to tell which of the two seas is deeper when in neither can soundings be found. (C. Adamson)

The Octopus is not only a fearsome deep-sea creature, but also a three-move Checker opening whose tentacles every player dreads. An excellent book on the Octopus Opening (10-15, 21-17, 7-10 . . . weak for Black) has been written by former American Champion Gene Frazier. (T.W.)

Odds Even

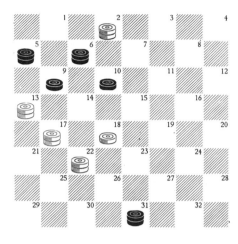

Problem No. 9
By Milton Johnson
BLACK: 9, 10, kings 5, 6, 31
WHITE: 18, kings 2, 13, 17, 22
White to play and draw

Solution

2-7 (necessary), 31-27, 7-14, 27-23, 22-26 (any other move is immediately fatal), 23-30, 17-21, 30-26, 14-17—A, 26-23, 18-14—B, 9-18, 17-14, 18-22 (else this checker is lost by 13-17, then 21-25), 14-9—C, 5-14, 13-17—D. Drawn.

A—Of course, if 13-17, 9-13, etc. Black wins.

B—If 17-14, 6-1, 13-6, 1-17, 21-14 (Black has "the move," and plays for the American Position win), 23-19, 14-10, 5-9, 10-7, 9-6, 7-3, 6-10, 18-15, 10-6, 15-11, 6-10, 11-8, 19-16, 8-4, 16-12, Black wins.

C—If 13-17, 22-25!, Black wins.

D—The late Milton Johnson was one of America's foremost problemists and a strong crossboard player as well.

Even as You and I

Dr. Marion Tinsley, Walter Hellman, Asa Long, Eugene Frazier, Edwin Hunt, Basil Case, Newell Banks, Everett Fuller—all great masters—have one thing in common. They have made some of the silliest mistakes while playing serious checkers. So, dear reader, take heart! (T.W.)

Trigger Shot

BLACK

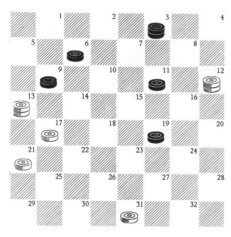

WHITE

Problem No. 10
By Milton Johnson
BLACK: 6, 9, 11, 19, king 3
WHITE: 17, 21, 31, kings 12, 13
White to play and draw

Solution

31-26—A, 3-7—B, 26-22, 11-15, 12-16—C, 19-23, 16-19—C, 15-24, 22-18, 7-11, 17-14, 11-15, 14-5—D, 15-22, 5-1—D, 6-10, 21-17—E, etc. Neatly drawn.

A—It looks bleak for White, but this move leads to a beautiful drawing combination worth your close attention.

B—How can White successfully invade enemy territory? That is the problem that must be solved.

C—White is about to make a key sacrifice that permits the necessary penetration of Black terrain.

D—Although still a man down, White's draw is now assured—though not without some fancy footwork.

E—Because Black cannot avoid the impending shot. If 10-15, 13-9; if 23-26 or 23-27, 1-6, etc. If 24-27 or 24-28, 1-6, etc. Drawn. This theme was first termed the "Trigger Shot" by the celebrated Julius D'Orio, of *Mysteries of Dama* fame.

BLACK

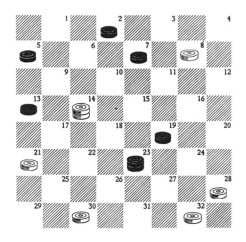

WHITE

Problem No. 11
By Jules Leopold and Jack Botte
BLACK: 2, 5, 7, 13, 19, king 23
WHITE: 8, 21, 28, 30, 32, king 14
White to play and win

Solution

8-3—A, 7-10—B, 14-7, 2-11, 3-7, 11-16—C, 7-11, 16-20, 11-16, 5-9, 32-27—D, 23-32, 16-23, 9-14, 30-25—E, 13-17, 23-26, 32-27, 26-31, 27-23, 28-24, 20-27, 31-24, 23-18, 24-19—F, 17-22, 19-15. White wins.

A—If 8-4, 19-24, 28-19, 23-16, 4-8, 16-11, 8-15, 7-10, etc. Draws.

B—7-11 gets the same idea: 7-11, 3-8, 11-16, 8-11, 16-20, 11-16, 2-6, 32-27, 23-32, 16-23, 6-9, 14-18, 9-14, 18-9, 5-14. White wins as shown.

C—11-15, 8-11, 23-18, 30-26, 5-9, 26-22, 18-25, 11-18, etc. White wins.

D—This move, and the next, may be transposed.

E—If 30-26, 13-17, 26-22, 17-26, 23-30, 32-27, 30-26, 20-24, 28-19, 27-23, drawn.

F—For the winning play against the forced 17-22 squeeze.

Easy Doesn't It

There is always an easy solution to every problem . . . neat, plausible and wrong! (H. L. Mencken)

Embryonic End-Game

BLACK

WHITE

Problem No. 12
Jules Leopold vs. Tom Wiswell
BLACK: 1, 4, 28
WHITE: 18, king 32
White to play and draw

Solution

18-15—A, 4-8—B, 15-10—A, 8-12, 10-7—A, 12-16, 7-2—A, 16-20, 2-7, 1-6, 7-11, 6-10, 11-16, 10-15, 16-11, 15-19, 11-16, 19-23, 16-19, 23-26, 19-15—C, 26-31, 15-19, 31-26, 19-15, 26-23, 15-10—D, 20-24, 10-15, 24-27, 15-11, 27-31, 11-16, 31-27, 16-20—E. Drawn.

A—White, although a man down, has legitimate hopes of obtaining a standard drawing position known to all experts and masters.

B—Better than 1-6 as it gets square 20 and, for a time, prevents White from gaining control of that vital square, the key to his draw.

C—Or 19-16—but not 19-24, 20-27, 32-30, 28-32, 30-26, 32-27. Black wins.

D—White has gained his objective: a standard position by W. Payne that draws when White has the opposition and can get, or control, square 20.

E—From a game between Leopold and Wiswell, played at The Chess & Checker Club of New York, April 12, 1971.

Aquarian

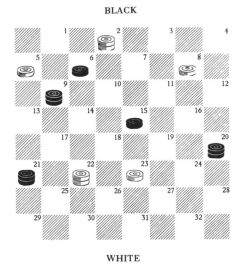

Problem No. 13
By Matt Long
BLACK: 6, 15, kings 9, 20, 21
WHITE: 5, 8, 23, kings 2, 22
White to play and win

Solution

5-1—A, 6-10, 23-18—B, 15-19, 18-15, 10-14, 22-17, 14-18, 1-5—C, 21-14, 15-10—D, 14-7, 5-16, 20-4, 2-11—E. White wins.

A—*Not* 23-18, 15-19, 5-1, 9-14!, etc., drawn.

B—*Not* 1-6, 9-14, etc., drawn. Nor 2-7, 9-5, drawn.

C—Now the point of White's maneuvering is apparent.

D—This theme was first exploited by the great Sturges early in the nineteenth century.

E—This "Aquarian" problem was an entry in Bill Salot's Problem Contest Number Two and was nosed out by Tom Wiswell's "Minority Rule" problem. However, Matt Long had the consolation of knowing that he was beaten by the "Problem Of The Year."

Boston Marathon?

Probably the longest game on record, in terms of how many moves were required, was played by A. H. Richardson and E. A. Durgin, two doughty draughts players of Massachusetts. Between them, the players made 228 moves.

While there is no record of the actual time consumed, under the standard rules it *could* have taken as much as 22 hours! (J. L.)

Perfect Parallelogram

BLACK

WHITE

Problem No. 14
By M.H.C. Wardell
BLACK: 23, 28, king 15
WHITE: 29, 32 king 22
Black to play and draw

Solution

15-11, 29-25, 11-16, 25-21, 16-20, 21-17, 20-24, 17-13, 24-27, 13-9—A, 27-31, 22-25, 31-26, 25-30 (White now has the Bridge Position he sought), 26-22—B, 9-6, 22-18, 6-2, 18-15—C, Drawn.

A—If 22-25, 27-31, 25-30, 31-27—D, etc. and Black again returns to square 15 and makes the sacrifice as shown under note C.

B—Returning into the Bridge loses: 26-31, 9-6, 31-27, 6-2, 27-24, 2-7, 24-27, 7-11, 27-24, 11-15 (not 11-16, then 23-26) 24-27, 30-25, 27-31 (if 27-24, 25-22), 15-19, 31-26, 19-24, 26-31, 25-30. White wins.

C—You can go home again! The Black king has completed his geometrical journey. Now 2-7, 23-27 breaking the Bridge, 32-23, 28-32 to regain the piece and draw. Well done, Mr. Wardell.

D—*Not* 31-26, 32-27, 23-32, 30-23. White wins.

What, Again?

There is no disgrace in losing a game of checkers; the only disgrace is in losing the same way twice! (T.W.)

Mighty Monarch

BLACK

WHITE

Problem No. 15
By Tom Wiswell and Howard Peck
BLACK: 2, 8, 11, 12, 15, kings 17, 32
WHITE: 9, 13, 18, 20, 22, 23, 28, 31
White to play and win

Solution

23-19, 15-24, 28-19, 17-26, 31-22, 32-27—A, 9-6, 2-9, 13-6, 27-23—B, 6-2!!, 23-14—C, 22-18!!, 14-16, 2-7—D, 11-15, 20-4, 15-19, 7-11, 19-24, 4-8, 24-28, 8-3, 28-32, 3-7, 32-27, 7-10, 27-24, 10-15—E, etc. White wins by First Position.

A—If 2-7, 18-14, 32-27, 22-18, etc., White wins.

B—27-31 and 27-24 also lose.

C—Of course, if 23-16, 2-7, White wins.

D—White, two men down, nevertheless wins the game.

E—A sensational yet very practical win . . . from the 9-13, 22-18, 10-15 opening.

Laird and Lady

This opening was named after the draughts-playing Scottish couple, Laird and Lady Cather. It is formed by these opening moves: 11-15, 23-19, 8-11, 22-17, 9-13, 17-14, and is a draw when properly played. However, if instead of 17-14, White moves 25-22, it is the Laird and Lady Refused—and White already has a lost game.

Hell hath no fury like a lady scorned! (J.L.)

Double Danger

BLACK

Problem No. 16
By Tom Wiswell and Jimmy Ricca
BLACK: 2, 6, 9, 10, king 23
WHITE: 11, 13, 15, 17, 19, 28
White to play and draw

WHITE

Solution

19-16, 10-19, 11-8, 23-26—A, 8-3, 26-22—A, 16-11 (necessary), 19-23, 28-24—B, 23-26, 24-19, 26-30—C, 19-15, 30-25—D, 3-7, 25-21, 17-14!, 9-18, 7-10, 6-9, 13-6, 2-9, 10-14—E. Drawn.

A—Black has his eye on the man on square 17 and White's problem is to prevent the loss of the piece.

B—The beginning of White's only drawing plan; all other moves lose.

C—If 26-31, 3-7, 31-27, 19-15, 27-24, (or 27-23), 15-10, etc. Drawn.

D—If 30-26, 3-7, 26-23, 15-10 draws but 7-10, 23-19, 10-1, 19-10, 13-6, 22-13, Black wins.

E—Black may vary from the above play but it does not help as White's draw is secure.

Looking Ahead

Don't be discouraged if "looking ahead" seems difficult at first. It gets easier the more you practice it. And I have found that one big secret of Checker success is this: When you think you have looked as far ahead as you can, or want to, *compel* yourself to visualize just one move more! (J.L.)

Perpetual Motion

BLACK

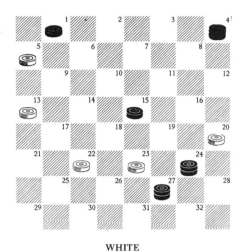

Problem No. 17
By Tom Wiswell
BLACK: 1, 15, kings 4, 24, 27
WHITE: 5, 13, 20, 22, 23
White to play and draw

WHITE

Solution

23-19—A, 15-18—B, 22-15, 27-23—C, 13-9—D, 23-16, 20-11, 24-19, 15-10, 19-15, 9-6, 15-8, 6-2, 8-3—E, 10-6!—F, 1-10, 2-7, 10-15 (or 10-14), 7-11, 15-19, 5-1, 19-24, 1-6, 24-27, 6-10, 27-32, 10-15, etc. Drawn by "perpetual check."

A—If 23-18, 15-19, 18-15, 4-8, 13-9, 19-23, 15-10, 8-3, etc. Black wins; White may vary but the Black kings are monarchs of all they survey.

B—Best, and *almost* wins for Black, but not quite.

C—Otherwise White draws with 13-9.

D—If 19-16 (20-16, 23-18, 16-11, 4-8), 24-19, 15-10, 19-12, Black wins.

E—If 8-11, 10-7 and if 8-12, 2-7, or 10-7. Drawn.

F—Necessary to break out of the Bridge Position, because if, instead, 2-6 (2-7, 1-6), 4-8, 6-9, 8-11, 9-6, 11-16, 6-9, 16-19, 9-6, 19-23, 6-9, 23-18, 9-6, 3-8, 6-2, 18-14, 2-7, 14-9, Black wins.

Skil[duggery

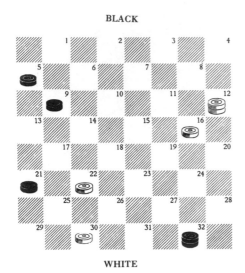

Problem No. 18
By Tom Wiswell
BLACK: 5, 9, 21, king 32
WHITE: 16, 22, 30, king 12
White to play and win

Solution

16-11—A, 32-27—B, 12-8—C, 9-13—D, 8-3, 5-9, 3-7, 9-14, 7-10, 14-17, 10-15—E, 17-26, 30-23, 27-18, 15-22. White wins.

A—Because 12-8, 9-13, 8-11, 5-9, 11-15, 9-14, etc. draws.

B—If 9-13, 12-16, 5-9, 16-19, 9-14, 19-23, etc., White wins. If 32-28, 12-16, etc., White wins.

C—If 11-7, 9-13, etc. draws, and if 12-16, 27-23, etc. draws.

D—Because 27-23, 8-3, 23-19, 3-7 and then 7-10, if 9-13 or 9-14.

E—Now it is apparent why it was necessary to keep the man on square 11.

Long, Long a Go

A single game of checkers between masters has been known to take as much as seven hours. But one chess game between Morphy and Paulsen took over 17 hours. However, all awards for board-game endurance must surely go to Go—the Japanese game of circumvention. I have it on good authority that two Go masters playing a single game were at it for over a week! (J.L.)

Escape Artist

Problem No. 19
By Tom Wiswell
BLACK: 7, 13, kings 8, 14
WHITE: 15, 23, kings 6, 30
White to play and draw

Solution

30-25—A, 7-11—B, 23-18!—C, 14-23, 6-10—C, 11-18, 10-15—D,
8-12—D, 15-22, 12-16, 25-30, 16-19, 30-25, 19-15, 25-30—E. Drawn.
A—The only move to draw. If 15-10, 7-11, 10-7, 14-10. Black wins. The
purpose of 30-25 will soon be apparent.
B—Black has nothing better; if 7-10, 23-19, 14-18, 15-11, draws.
C—Now White's plan for an unusual escape begins to unfold. Watch how that
king on square 6 gets into the action.
D—Black's only practical moves are with one of his kings and they all permit
White to escape via . . .
E—. . . our old friend, Payne's Draw, standard "man-down" ending.

Long Time No Solve!

The "Hundred Years Problem" was so named because analysts worked on it
through a period of 100 years before a definite solution was reached. Yet it
involved only five pieces per side! (See page 125 of Boland's *Masterpieces in
the Game of Checkers*.)

BLACK

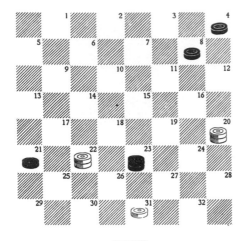

WHITE

Problem No. 20
By Tom Wiswell
BLACK: 4, 8, 21, king 23
WHITE: 31, kings 20, 22
White to play and draw

Solution

31-26—A, 23-30, 20-16, 8-11—B, 16-7, 4-8, 7-10, 8-11, 10-14, 11-15, 14-10, 15-19, 10-15, 19-24, 15-19, 24-27, 19-23, 27-32—C, 22-25—D, 32-28, 25-22, 28-24, 22-25, 24-20, 25-22, 20-16, 22-25, 16-11, 25-22, 11-15, 22-25, 30-26—E, 23-30, 15-18, 25-22—F, 18-25, 30-26. Drawn.

A—White, already one down, gives up another man to assure the draw. If 20-16, 23-26, 22-25 (22-17, 8-12), 21-30, 31-22, 30-26, 22-18, 26-23, 18-15, 23-27!, 15-10, 27-24, 10-6, 24-20, etc., Black wins.

B—Best. If 21-25 (8-12, 16-11), 22-29, 30-26, 29-25, 26-23, 25-22, 23-27, 22-18, 27-24, 18-15, etc., draws.

C—If 27-31, 22-25, 31-26, 23-27, etc., draws.

D—White's strategy for drawing, despite everything.

E—Black's last hope and it *does* look promising for a moment.

F—However, this sacrifice, based on fundamental principles, holds the draw that White foresaw as far back as Note A.

Decisions, Decisions, Decisions

All good players employ the process of elimination. So, don't snap at the first likely move that meets your eye. (T.W.)

Grand Illusion

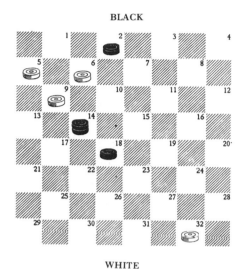

Problem No. 21
By Tom Wiswell
BLACK: 2, 18, king 14
WHITE: 5, 6, 9, 32
White to play and draw

Solution

32-27—A, 18-22—B, 27-23, 22-26, 23-18!—C, 14-23, 5-1!—D, 23-18, 1-5, 18-14, 6-1, 26-30, 1-6, 30-26, 6-1, 26-23, 1-6, 23-19 (if 23-18, 6-10), 6-1, 19-15, 1-6—E, etc. Drawn.

A—Necessary, if 6-1, 14-10, 32-27, 18-22, 27-23, 22-26, 23-19, 26-31, 19-15 (If 19-16, 31-26, etc., Black wins), 10-19, 1-6, 19-15, 5-1, 31-26, 1-5, 26-23, 6-1, 15-18, 1-6, 18-14, 6-1, 23-18. Black wins.

B—14-10, 5-1, 18-22, 27-23, 22-26, 23-19, 26-31, 19-15, 10-19, 1-5. Drawn.

C—Easing the Black grip on the Double-Corner men and allowing White to maneuver, even though still locked in.

D—Not 6-1, 23-18, 1-6, 18-14, 6-1, 14-10, etc. Black wins.

E—Black does not have "the move." With it he would win here. Despite the fact that Black is a man down in the above diagram it appears that White is lost, but this is only an illusion. Often the right combination of moves can transform an apparent defeat into a logical draw—or even a win!

Back Against the Wall

BLACK

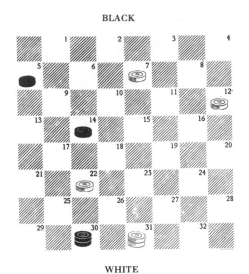

Problem No. 22
By Tom Wiswell
BLACK: 5, 14, king 30
WHITE: 7, 12, 22, king 31
White to play and win

WHITE

Solution

7-2—A, 30-25, 22-17, 14-21, 31-26, 5-9, 12-8—B, 9-13, 26-30, 25-22, 2-6—C, 22-18, 8-3—D, 13-17, 3-7—D, 17-22—E, 7-10, 18-23—F, 10-14—G, 22-26 (22-25, 14-17 wins as in Variation F), 14-18!, 23-14, 30-23, 14-17, 23-26, 21-25, 26-30, 25-29, 6-10, etc. White wins.

A—If 12-8, 5-9, 7-2 (or 8-3), 9-13, followed by 30-25. Drawn.

B—Necessary. If 2-7, 9-13, 26-30, 25-22, 7-10, 22-18, 12-8, 13-17, 8-3, 17-22, 3-7, 22-25, 7-2, 18-23 (25-29, 30-26), 10-14, 25-29, 14-17, 29-25, 2-6, 23-27, 6-9, 27-31, draws.

C—Or White can play 8-3. However, once he gains this square it must not be relinquished—at least for some time.

D—This king must go to 14 to consummate the win.

E—If 18-14, 7-2, 14-18, 6-10, 17-22 (18-14, 30-26) 2-6 same as trunk of solution.

F—22-25, 6-9, 25-29, 9-13, 29-25, 13-17, 18-23 (18-14, 10-15), 10-14, 23-27, 14-18, 27-32, 17-22, 25-29, 18-23, 32-28, 23-27, 28-32, 22-26, 32-23, 26-19, 29-25, 30-26. White wins.

G—Necessary. 10-15 is wasted motion: 10-15, 23-18, 15-10 is the same. (If 15-19 or 15-11, in reply to 23-18, then 18-14 etc. draws.)

The Spoiler

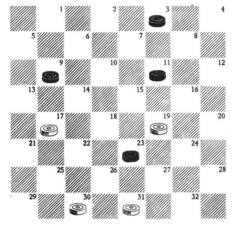

Problem No. 23
By Tom Wiswell
BLACK: 3, 9, 11, 23
WHITE: 17, 19, 30, 31
White to play and win

WHITE

Solution

17-13—A, 9-14, 13-9, 3-8—B, 9-6, 8-12, 6-2, 11-16, 2-7, 16-20—C, 7-10—D, 14-17, 10-14, 17-21, 19-16—F, 12-19, 14-18, etc. White wins.
A—Four-by-four settings, where the strength is almost equal, are often very instructive and fascinating.
B—Of course, 3-7, 9-6, 7-10, 6-2, etc. White wins easily.
C—If 23-27, 31-24, 16-23, 7-10, 14-17, 10-14, 17-21, 24-20, etc. White wins. A standard ending related to First Position.
D—If 7-11, 23-27, 31-24, 20-27, etc., draws.
E—Just when Black thinks he has made the grade, White makes a timely sacrifice that wins handily. It reminds me of the following position I had with the late Prof. W. R. Fraser when I defended my title in our 1960 match: Black—2, 6, 12, 14, 20, 24. White (Wiswell)—15, 19, 21, 31, 32, king 3. White to play. I went 15-11, 14-18, 3-8, 18-23, 11-7, 2-11, 8-15, 6-9, 21-17, 9-13, 17-14, 13-17, 19-16 (the spoiler), 12-19, 15-18, 17-21, 18-27, 21-25, 32-28, 25-30, 27-32. White wins. This virtually clinched the match for me.

Journey's End

Problem No. 24
By Tom Wiswell
BLACK: 20, kings 24, 29, 31
WHITE: 30, kings 15, 18, 22
White to play and win

Solution

18-23, 24-28, 15-19, 28-32, 30-25, 31-27—A, 23-18, 32-28, 25-21, 20-24, 21-17, 27-32, 22-26, 29-25, 17-14, 32-27—B, 26-31, 27-32—C, 14-10, 32-27, 10-6, 27-32, 6-2, 32-27, 2-6, 27-32, 18-23, 25-22, 6-10, 22-17, 31-26, 17-21, 10-14, 21-25, 14-18, 25-30, 26-31, 30-25, 18-15—D. White wins.

A—Or Black may just shuttle back and forth and say "Come and get me". 32-28, 25-21, 28-32, 21-17, 32-28, 17-14, 28-32, 14-10, 32-28, 10-6, 28-32, 6-2, 32-28, 2-7, 28-32, 19-24 (now or later), 20-27, 7-11, 32-28, 23-32, 28-24, 11-15, 24-28, 15-19. White wins.

B—If 25-21, 18-22, etc. White wins easily. If 25-30, 19-15. White wins.

C—If 25-30, 19-23, 28-32, 14-9, 30-25, 18-14, 27-18, 14-23. White wins.

D—There are other ways of playing it but White can win in all variations. Played October 26, 1971, in a short match with Jack Botte.

Mastery

The problem of mastering Checkers can be mastered by mastering problems—and mastering openings. (T.W.)

Rhythm

BLACK

Problem No. 25
By Tom Wiswell
BLACK: 13, 21, kings 22, 31
WHITE: 10, 16, 19, 30, king 5
Black to play, White to win

WHITE

Solution

22-18—A, 10-7—B, 18-23—C, 5-9—D, 31-27, 16-11—E, 23-16, 7-3—E,
16-7, 3-10, 13-17—F, 30-26—G, 21-25—H, 26-23!, 27-18, 10-14, 17-22,
14-23, 25-30, 9-14, 22-25, 14-17, 25-29, 17-21—I. White wins.

A—Black, a man down, must seek to equalize the position.
B—Every White play is a star move; that means it is a must.
C—Getting a good grip on these two men gives Black hope.
D—Anything else will allow a draw as the timing is precise.
E—Seems to permit Black to escape—but watch!
F—If 27-23, 10-15, 23-27 (13-17, 9-14), 15-18, 27-32, 18-22. White wins.
G—The key to the White plan, a surprise move that might easily be missed.
H—If 27-31, 9-13, 31-22, 10-14 ties Black into a knot.
I—Perfect rhythm—a lesson in timing! End result, the American Position.

Imagination

What feeling, knowledge, or will man has depends in the last resort upon
what imagination he has. (Søren Kierkegaard)

Indirect Attack

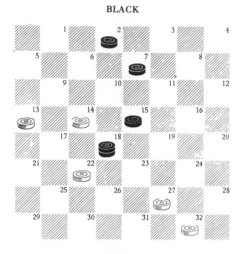

BLACK

WHITE

Problem No. 26
By Tom Wiswell
BLACK: 2, 7, 15, king 18
WHITE: 13, 14, 22, 27, 32
White to play and win

Solution

22-17—A, 18-9, 13-6, 2-9, 17-13—B, 9-14, 13-9—B, 14-18—C, 9-6, 7-11, 27-24—D, 11-16, 6-2, 16-19—E, 2-7—F, 19-28, 7-11!—G, 15-19, 11-15, 18-23, 15-24, 23-26, 24-19. White wins.

A—The only move to win and leads to an instructive theme.

B—Will the White king be in time? It doesn't look like it.

C—Lining up to exchange; if 7-10, 9-6, 14-17, 6-2, 10-14, 2-6, 15-18, 6-9, 17-21, 27-23, 18-27, 9-18, 27-31, 18-22. White wins.

D—Necessary. If 6-2, 18-23, 27-18, 15-22, etc. only draws.

E—If 18-23, 24-20, 16-19, 2-7, 19-24, 7-11, 15-19, 32-28. White wins.

F—24-20. 18-22, 2-7, 15-18, 7-10, 19-23, etc. only draws.

G—The student should note that the direct attack by 7-10 allows 18-22, 10-19, 22-26, drawn. The subtlety of this indirect waiting maneuver often escapes the grasp of the beginner. Note well, as the idea frequently arises in crossboard play.

Position Power

Problem No. 27
By Tom Wiswell
BLACK: 4, 5, 24, 27, 28
WHITE: 14, 31, kings 1, 19
White to play and win

Solution

1-6—A, 27-32 (best), 19-23—B, 4-8, 6-10, 8-11, 14-9—C, 5-14, 10-17, 11-16, 17-22, 16-20, 22-26, 24-27, 31-24, 20-27, 26-31—D. White wins.
A—If 19-23, 28-32, 1-6, 4-8, 6-10, 8-11, 14-9 (23-19, 32-28, 10-7, 11-16), 5-14, 10-17, 11-16, 17-22, 16-19, 23-16, 32-28, 16-19, 27-32, 22-18, 32-27, draws.
B—Necessary, and forces Black in a 'mating' net.
C—If 10-7, 11-16, 7-11, 16-20, 11-16, 24-27, 31-24, 20-27, 16-20, 27-31, 20-24, 32-27, 23-32, 31-26, 24-19, 26-22, 19-15, 22-17, 15-10, 17-13, 10-6, 13-17, 14-10, 17-14, 10-7, 14-18, 6-10, 18-23, 10-15, 5-9, 6-2, 9-13, etc., draws.
D—A good example of "position power." Such ideas can arise in play, usually to be overlooked by the players! Now and then, however, a wide-eyed critic is on hand to work out the win (or draw) for future generations of players.

Reason Prevails

Never make a move without a reason. Should your reason prove wrong, you will nonetheless have learned something. (J. L.)

Gamesmanship

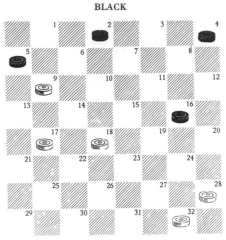

Problem No. 28
By Tom Wiswell
BLACK: 2, 4, 5, 16
WHITE: 9, 17, 18, 28, 32
White to play and win

Solution

17-14—A, 16-19 (If 4-8, 28-24), 28-24!—B, 19-28, 18-15, 4-8 (If 2-7, 9-6),
15-10, 8-12, 10-6, 12-16 (2-7, 6-2), 6-1, 16-19, 1-6, 19-23, 6-10, 23-26,
10-15, 26-31, 15-18, 31-26—C, 9-6, 2-9, 18-15—D. White wins.
A—If 18-14, 16-19, 32-27 (if 17-13, 19-23), 4-8, 27-24, 19-23, 24-19,
8-11, 28-24, 23-26, 24-20, 26-31, 19-16, 31-26 (or 11-15), 16-7, 2-11, 9-6,
26-22, 17-13, 22-17, 14-10, 17-14, etc., draws.
B—If 18-15 (32-27, 19-23), 19-23, 15-10, 23-26, 10-6, 26-30, 6-1, 30-26,
1-6, 26-22, 28-24 (6-10, 22-17), 22-17, 14-10, 5-14, 6-9, 14-18, 9-14, 2-7,
14-21, 7-14, 21-25, 14-17, 25-30, 17-22, 24-19 (32-27, 4-8), 18-23, 19-15,
22-26, 15-11, 26-31, 11-7, 31-26, 7-3, 26-22, etc., draws.
C—If 2-7, 18-22, 7-11, 9-6, 11-16, 6-2, 16-19, 2-6, 19-23, 6-9, 31-27
(23-26, 9-13, 26-30, 14-10), 9-13, 27-24, 13-17, etc. to a Bridge Position
where White wins.
D—A good lesson in gamesmanship in Checkers. Black may vary, of course,
but White can win against all lines of play.

The Strangler

BLACK

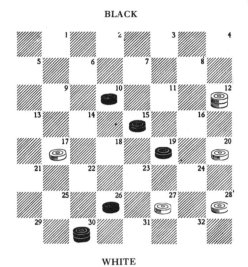

Problem No. 29
By Tom Wiswell
BLACK: 10, 15, 19, 26, king 30
WHITE: 17, 20, 27, 28, king 12
White to play and win

WHITE

Solution

17-14!—A, 10-17, 12-16!—B, 17-21 (or 17-22), 16-23, 21-25, 20-16, 25-29—C, 16-11, 29-25, 11-7, 25-21, 7-2, 21-17—C, 2-7, 17-14—C, 7-11, 15-18, 11-15, 18-22, 15-18!—D. White wins.

A—The sacrifice is necessary; if 27-24, 26-31, 12-8, 19-23, 8-11, 15-18, 11-7 (24-19, 30-25), 10-15, 7-11 (7-10, 30-25), 31-26, 17-14, 23-27, 14-9, 26-23, 9-6, 30-25, threatening 18-22. Drawn.

B—A strange situation. Black is one ahead but eventually must give up two men in return for the loan.

C—Black has very little choice at these points, due to White's strangle hold on the position.

D—White finally captures the second man, the inevitable consequence of the initial sacrifice at Note A.

Nice Doggie!

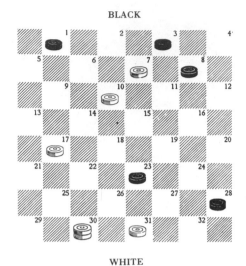

Problem No. 30
By Tom Wiswell
BLACK: 1, 3, 8, 23, 28
WHITE: 7, 10, 17, 31, king 30
White to play and win

Solution

7-2, 8-12 (1-5, 2-6), 2-7, 12-16—A, 7-11, 16-20, 31-26—B, 23-27, 10-6!, 1-10, 17-14!, 10-17, 26-22, 17-26, 30-32, 20-24, 11-16, 3-7—C, 16-20, 7-10—D, 20-27, 10-14, 27-23. White wins.

A—3-8 (1-6 no better), 7-3, 8-11, 3-8, 11-16, 8-11, 16-20, 31-26, 23-27, 11-16, 12-19, 26-23, 19-26, 30-32. White wins.

B—White now goes a man down to force an instructive win.

C—Because 24-27, 32-23, 28-32, White wins by First Position.

D—Black is damned if he does and damned if he doesn't. Usually where the choice is available, one or the other will get you "the move"—either pitching or letting your opponent jump. But here, because of the Dog-Hole effect, White winds up with the winning opposition, regardless!

Christy Matthewson

Christy Matthewson was one of the greatest baseball pitchers of all time. He was even a greater checker player—well, at least he could play checkers blindfolded, which is more than you could say of his pitching! (J.L.)

Attack and Defense

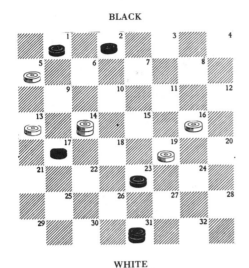

Problem No. 31
By Tom Wiswell
BLACK: 1, 2, 17, 23, king 31
WHITE: 5, 13, 16, 19, king 14
Black to play, White to draw

Solution

31-27—A, 14-21, 27-24, 19-15, 24-19, 15-10 (necessary), 19-12, 21-17, 12-8, 13-9 (17-14, 2-6), 8-3, 17-13, 2-7—B, 9-6, 7-14, 13-9, 1-10, 9-27—C. Drawn.

A—A good try by Black; if 17-21, 14-9, 31-27, 19-15, 27-24, 15-10, 24-19, 16-12, 19-15, 9-6, 2-9, 13-6, 15-11, 6-2, etc. Drawn.

B—If 23-27, 10-6 (*not* into the Bridge by 9-6), 1-10, 9-6, 2-9, 13-15. Drawn.

C—A simple example of 'attack and defense' in the end game that illustrates still another idea that may save a game for you in the future.

Early Curtains!

It is possible for Black's game to become irretrievably lost after he has made only three moves—seemingly harmless ones at that. One way: 11-16, 23-18, 16-20, 24-19, 8-11 (loses . . . by 19-15, 10-19, 18-14, 9-18, 22-8, 4-11 27-24.) Another way: 10-15, 23-19, 6-10, 22-17, 11-16 (loses . . . by 17-13, 16-23, 13-6, 2-9, 27-2). White, too, can lose in three moves by a trap similar to the latter: 10-14, 23-19, 11-16, 26-23, 9-13, 24-20 (loses . . . by 14-17, 21-14, 6-10, 20-11, 10 26, 31-22, 8-31.) (J.L.)

Double Exposure

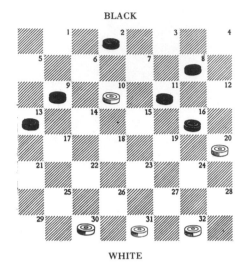

BLACK

WHITE

Problem No. 32
By Tom Wiswell
BLACK: 2, 8, 9, 11, 13, 16
WHITE: 10, 20, 30, 31, 32
White to play and win

Solution

10-7, 8-12, 7-3, 2-7, 3-10, 9-14, 10-17, 13-22, 30-26—A, 22-25, 26-23—A, 25-30, 32-28, 30-25, 31-26, 25-30—B, 28-24, 30-25, 23-18—C, 25-30—D, 26-23, 30-26, 24-19, 26-22, 19-15—E. White wins.

A—White allows Black to get a king, and thereby wins, as you shall see.

B—If 25-21, 28-24, 21-17, 23-18, etc. White wins, as above.

C—*Not* 24-19, 25-30, 26-22, 11-15, 19-10, 30-25. Drawn.

D—Again 25-21, 26-23, etc. still wins for White.

E—Timing, and the fact that Black has two men exposed simultaneously, overcomes the power of the king. Not spectacular, perhaps, but worthy of note by the student.

Believe It or Not

Even the late Bob Ripley—who was evidently not a checker buff—thought that a game was declared a draw when one player was so blocked as to be unable to move. His erroneous verdict of "draw" was appended to the following block game that appeared in his "Believe It or Not" feature. Tom Wiswell then wrote him to advise that it was actually a White win: 10-15, 23-18, 12-16, 21-17, 9-13, 24-20, 16-19, 17-14, 6-9, 27-24, 1-6, 32-27, 8-12, 25-21, 12-16, 27-23, 6-10 (7-10 here will draw), 21-17, 4-8, 29-25, 8-12, 25-21, 3-8, 30-25, 2-6, 31-27.

Death Grip

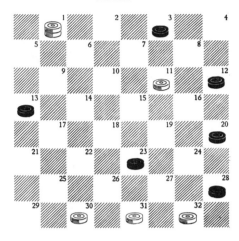

Problem No. 33
By Tom Wiswell
BLACK: 3, 12, 13, 20, 23, 28
WHITE: 11, 30, 31, 32, king 1
White to play and win

Solution

31-27—A, 23-26—B, 30-23, 13-17, 1-6—C, 17-22, 11-7—D, 3-10, 6-15, 22-26, 15-19, 26-31—E, 27-24!—F, 20-27, 19-24!—G, 12-16, 24-19!—H, 16-20, 19-24!—I. White wins.

A—If 1-6, 20-24, 11-7, 3-10, 6-15, 23-27, 32-23, 12-16, etc. draws.

B—Black's best chance. Otherwise White wins the Bridge position with ease.

C—Preparing for the exchange that is necessary to gain the win.

D—6-10, 22-26, 10-15, 26-31, 27-24, 20-27, 15-19, 31-26, 19-24. Drawn.

E—26-30, 23-18, 30-26, 18-15, 26-31, 19-24, 31-26, 15-11, etc. White wins.

F—White pitches and gets a fatal grip; if 19-24, 12-16, etc. draws.

G—Black has a few gasps left, but all to no avail.

H—*Not* 24-20, 16-19, 23-16, 31-26, 32-23, 26-12. Black wins.

I—From a "Pioneer" opening. The winning procedure was found after the game had ended in a draw.

Fool's Gold

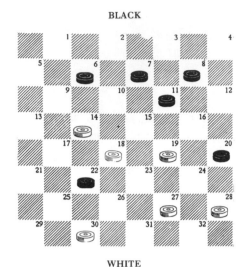

Problem No. 34
By Tom Wiswell
BLACK: 6, 7, 8, 11, 20, 22
WHITE: 14, 18, 19, 27, 28, 30
Black to play and draw

Solution

6-10, 19-16—A, 10-17, 16-12, 11-16!—C, 12-3, 16-19!—C, 3-10, 19-23!—C, 10-14, 23-32, 14-21, 32-27!—D. Drawn.

A—Appears to be a certain White win, but it's only fool's gold. If 14-9, 8-12, 9-6 (27-23, 11-16, 9-6, etc. Same), 11-16, 27-23, 22-26, 6-1—B, 26-31, 1-6, 10-14, 18-9, 31-27, draws.

B—*Not* 6-2, 26-31, 2-11, 20-24, 11-27, 31-22. Black wins!

C—Black resigned this position in the game and I happened to spy the draw from the sidelines.

D—Based on a Single Corner game played at The New York Club on August 30, 1974. The lesson for today might well be: Never resign; always re-sign.

The Paradoxical Twins

Do you know that sometimes an uncrowned man may be better than a king? Place White on 16, king on 6. Place Black on 3, 4, and 8. Now White moves, and he can win. But if you change the White man on 16 to a king, the position is only a draw! (J.L.)

An Ancient Art

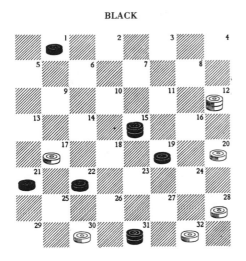

BLACK

WHITE

Problem No. 35
By Tom Wiswell
BLACK: 1, 19, 21, 22, kings 15, 31
WHITE: 17, 20, 28, 30, 32, king 12
White to play and win

Solution

32-27—A, 31-24, 12-16—A, 1-6 (best), 16-23, 6-10, 28-19, 15-24, 23-18, 22-25, 17-13, 25-29, 13-9, 10-14, 18-22, 24-19, 9-6, 19-15, 6-2 (or 6-1), 14-18—B, 20-16—C, 18-25, 16-11, 15-8, 2-7—D. White wins.

A—Eventually leads to one of the oldest themes in problem lore.

B—Black can delay this, but to no avail.

C—Probably the type of play most apt to be overlooked by students.

D—Always look for that extra twist in your endings. You'll be pleasantly surprised how often you'll find it.

Two Tough!

One of the most difficult problems on the checkerboard has only two pieces on each side! Its composer is Dr. Brown, famous for his numerous two-by-two posers.

Black man on 7, king on 20. White kings on 31 and 32. White to move and win.

The variations are too numerous to show here, but I can tell you this much: White *must* begin by moving the king on 32, otherwise his win is gone with the wind! (J.L.)

Deadwood

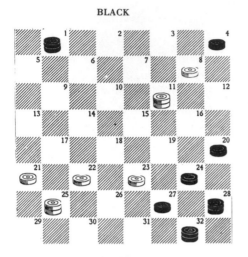

Problem No. 36
By Tom Wiswell
BLACK: 4, 20, 24, 27, kings 1, 28, 32
WHITE: 8, 21, 22, 23, kings 11, 25
White to play and win

Solution

22-17—A, 1-6—B, 17-14, 6-1—B, 21-17, 1-6, 17-13, 6-1, 13-9, 1-5, 9-6, 5-1, 6-2, 1-5, 2-6, 5-1, 14-10, 1-5, 10-7, 5-1, 6-10, 1-5, 7-2, 5-1 (5-9, 2-7), 2-6, 1-5, 10-14, 5-1, 6-9, 27-31—C, 11-15!, 4-27, 25-22—D, 1-5, 9-6, 5-1, 14-10, 1-5, 6-1, 5-9, 1-5, 9-13, 10-14, 13-9, 14-17, 9-6, 5-9—E, 6-13, 17-14—F. White wins.

A—The key move as it prevents 27-31. See note B.
B—Because if 27-31, 11-15 wins as shown above at note C.
C—Forced as 1-5 loses by 14-18, 5-14, 18-9, etc.
D—The pesky King on one must still be cornered to chalk up the win.
E—White is generous to the last . . . with the worst of intentions.
F—Jack Botte observed that "Black is left with nothing but deadwood," and we think that is as good a title as any. Thanks, Jack!

Learned Counsel

If you've learned how you can lose you've learned as much as the player who has learned how he can win. (T.W.)

Something Old, Something New

BLACK

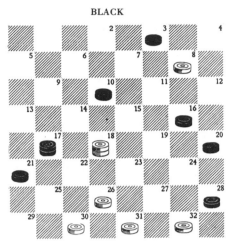

WHITE

Problem No. 37
By Tom Wiswell
BLACK: 3, 10, 16, 20, 21, 28, king 17
WHITE: 8, 26, 30, 31, 32, king 18
White to play and win

Solution

18-22 (necessary), 3-12, 22-13, 10-15, 13-17, 15-19—A, 17-22, 19-24, 26-23!—B, 24-27, 31-24, 20-27, 23-19!—C, 16-23, 22-26!—C, 21-25 (best chance), 26-19, 25-29—D, 32-23, 28-32, 23-18—E. White wins.

A—Black heads for square 24, his only hope.

B—White gives Black just what he wants—with an ulterior motive.

C—And this was the motive.

D—Because 27-31, 30-21, 31-26, 21-17, etc. White wins.

E—A standard win, with or without "the move." I continue for the benefit of the student: 32-27, 18-14, 27-32, 14-9, 32-27, 9-6, 27-32, 6-2, 32-27, 2-6, 27-32, 6-10, 32-27, 10-14, 27-32, 14-18, 32-27, 18-22, 27-32, 19-24, 32-28 (12-16, 22-26), 24-27, 12-16, 22-26, 16-20, 27-32, 28-24, 26-23, etc. White wins.

Crowning Insult

Your newly acquired king deserves to be crowned—*immediately*. And the rules require your opponent to do it, not you. As for the player who persistently ignores this rule—he deserves to be crowned too! (T.W.)

Machiavellian

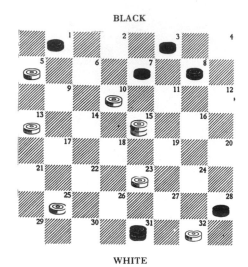

WHITE

Problem No. 38
By Tom Wiswell
BLACK: 1, 3, 7, 8, 28, king 31
WHITE: 5, 10, 13, 23, 25, 32, king
15
White to play and win

Solution

15-18—A, 7-14, 18-9, 31-26, 23-19, 8-11, 9-14, 26-23, 19-15—A, 11-18, 32-27, 23-32, 14-23, 3-8, 13-9 (or 25-22), 8-12, 25-22, 12-16, 22-18, 16-20, 18-15—B, 20-24, 15-10, 24-27, 9-6, 27-31, 6-2, 31-27, 2-7— C, 27-18, 10-6—C, 1-10, 7-23—C. White wins.

A—White begins a series of forced moves worthy of the ancient Prince of Politics, for whom the position is named.

B—If 9-6, 1-10, 5-1, 20-24, 1-6, 10-15, 18-11, 24-27, 6-10, 27-31, etc. Drawn.

C—Looks like a composition but is based on actual play.

The Roots of Wisdom

In Checkers, as in life, if there were no aftermath there would be no progress. The wisdom of today is the ignorance of yesterday, classified in the storehouse of knowledge for the use of tomorrow. (Joseph Maize)

Modus Operandi

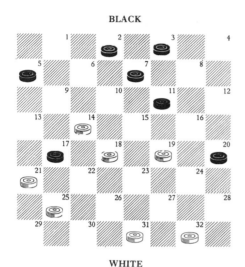

Problem No. 39
By Tom Wiswell
BLACK: 2, 3, 5, 7, 11, 17, 20
WHITE: 14, 18, 19, 21, 25, 31, 32
White to play and draw

Solution

25-22 (if 31-26, 11-15), 17-26, 31-22, 2-6—A, 22-17, 20-24, 19-15—B, 3-8, 32-28—C, 24-27, 28-24, 27-31, (if 11-16, 24-19) 24-20, 31-26, 17-13, 26-22, (if 26-23, 14-9, or if 26-30, 13-9), 15-10, 6-15, 20-16—D. Drawn.

A—If 20-24, 22-17, 2-6, etc. same as above solution.

B—White may transpose moves here but the mode of operation is essential to the draw.

C—Note that 17-13 allows Black to get in 11-16, etc.

D—From an 11-15, 22-17, 8-11 opening played April 1, 1972, in a ten-game match with Connecticut Champion Howard Peck, one of my favorite sparring partners.

Longevity

We have it on the word of one mathematician that 40 million people, each playing one game every ten minutes for ten hours a day and 300 days a year, would take 1,600,279 years to play all the variations in Checkers.

Meanwhile, who would be tending the store? (J.L.)

No Exit

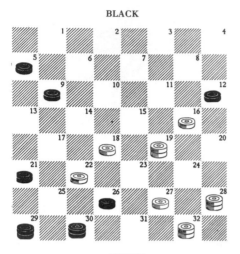

BLACK

WHITE

Problem No. 40
By Tom Wiswell
BLACK: 5, 9, 12, 21, 26, kings 29, 30
WHITE: 16, 18, 22, 27, kings 19, 28, 32
White to play and win

Solution

18-14! (necessary), 9-25, 27-24—A, 5-9—B, 32-27, 9-14—B, 27-32—C, 26-31—D, 19-23!, 12-26, 32-27—E, 14-18, 27-23—F, 18-27, 28-32!—F. White wins.

A—*Not* 27-23, 5-9, 32-27, 9-14, 27-32 (27-31, 14-17), 14-18, 23-14, 27-31, 19-23, 12-26, 28-24, 31-27, 24-22, 30-26, 22-31, 25-30. Drawn.

B—If 26-31, 19-23, etc. White wins as in trunk play shown above.

C—If 27-31, 14-17, or 14-18, etc., draws.

D—Because if 14-18, 19-15, 12-19, 15-31, etc. White wins.

E—White still has a last holdout with which to contend.

F—The final indignity which leaves the opposition with 'No Exit'.

Persistence Pays

Remember, today's champion first began as a lowly loser, gradually became a top drawer, and finally developed into a big winner. Nothing succeeds like . . . persistence. (J.L.)

The Sting

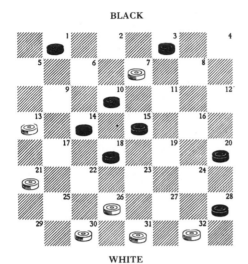

BLACK

WHITE

Problem No. 41
By Tom Wiswell
BLACK: 1, 3, 10, 14, 15, 18, 20, 28
WHITE: 7, 13, 21, 26, 30, 31, 32
White to play and win

Solution

7-2, 18-23—A, 26-19, 15-24, 2-6—B, 3-7 (10-15, 6-10), 6-15, 7-10, 15-6, 1-10, 13-9—C, 10-15, 9-6, 15-18—D, 21-17!—E, 14-21, 31-26, etc. White wins.

A—As good as anything at Black's disposal.

B—If 2-7, 24-27, 32-23, 14-18! and Black escapes.

C—Or White can transpose here with 31-26, 10-15, 13-9, etc., same as the above solution. However, if 26-22 (after 10-15), 14-18, 22-17, 18-23, 13-9, 24-27, 9-6, 27-31, 6-2, 23-27, 32-23, 31-27 (breaking the Bridge). Drawn.

D—Black thinks he will surely draw now—but the game is never over until the last 'out'.

E—This instructive sacrifice effectively nullifies Black's hope of a draw. If, instead of 21-17, White plays 31-26, 24-27, 32-23, 18-27, 26-22, 27-31, 6-2, 28-32, 2-6, 32-27, 6-9, 14-18, 22-15, 31-26, draws.

Super Man

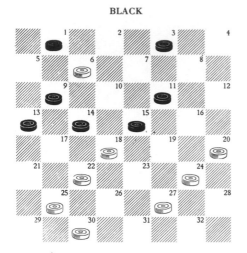

BLACK

WHITE

Problem No. 42
By Tom Wiswell
BLACK: 1, 3, 9, 11, 13, 14, 15
WHITE: 6, 18, 20, 22, 24, 25, 27, 30
White to play and draw

Solution

27-23, 1-10, 25-21, 3-8—A, 20-16—B, 11-27, 18-4, 10-15, 4-8, 27-31, 8-11!—C, 31-26, 11-18, 26-19, 18-23!!—D, 19-17, 30-26—E. Drawn.

A—There is no threat in 3-7; this poses a problem, however.

B—*Not* 23-19, 14-23, 19-16, 9-14, 16-7, 14-17, 21-14, 10-26, 7-3, 8-12, 3-7, 26-31, 7-11, 15-18, 11-15, 18-22, 15-18, 31-27, 18-25, 23-26, 30-23, 27-18, 25-30 (24-19, 13-17), 18-15, 30-26, 13-17, 26-23, 17-21, 23-27, 21-25, 27-32, 25-30, 32-28, 15-11, etc. Black wins.

C—Stepping into Black's 'trap'—with full knowledge.

D—The double sacrifice leads to an instructive and unusual finish; the 'super man' on 26 holds the king and three men at bay.

E—From an ending with New Jersey champion Jack Botte, played October 11, 1971.

Call to Battle

W. T. Call, author of *Midget Problems* and other checker books, estimated that there are 16 billion possible positions that can arise before a king is obtained.

Perpetual Check

BLACK

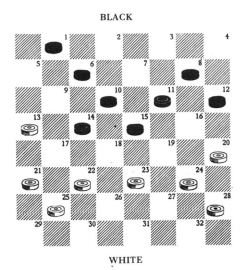

WHITE

Problem No. 43
By Tom Wiswell
BLACK: 1, 6, 8, 10, 11, 12, 14, 15
WHITE: 13, 20, 21, 22, 23, 24, 25,
     28

White to play and draw

Solution

24-19—A, 15-24, 28-19, 11-15, 22-17—B, 15-24, 25-22—B, 1-5 (best),
22-18—B, 5-9, 18-15—B, 10-26, 17-1, 9-14, 1-6, 14-18, 6-10, 18-23,
10-15—C, 24-28—D, 13-9, 28-32, 9-6, 32-28, 6-2, 28-24, 2-6—E, 26-31,
6-10, 24-28, 10-7, 28-24, 7-10, etc. Drawn.

A—This may look bad but White has a drawing plan well worked out.

B—This attack on the Black "elbow" is very instructive and saves the day for
White.

C—The White King is "monarch of all he surveys" and Black is never able to
approach with any safety. This type of draw arises from many games. I had this
ending in a "Cross" opening (11-15, 23-18) game with Phil Schwartzberg of
New York City.

D—Black may try many other ways of attacking, but to no avail.

E—White maintains a perpetual check on the Black piece on square 8. Note
the many squares Black must avoid. Also note why White must avoid 2-7 at
this point.

Firstest With the Mostest!

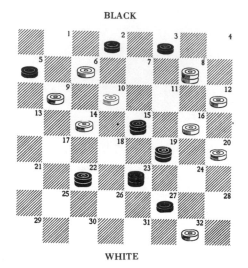

Problem No. 44
By Tom Wiswell
BLACK: 2, 3, 5, 27, kings 15, 19, 22, 23
WHITE: 6, 9, 10, 12, 14, 16, 20, 32, king 8
White to play and win

Solution

8-11—A, 15-8, 16-11—A, 8-15, 12-8—A, 3-12, 10-7—B, 2-11, 14-10—C, 5-14, 6-1—D, 15-6, 1-26—E, 23-30, 32-7, 30-26, 7-2, 26-23, 2-6, 23-19, 6-10—F. White wins.

A—White must clear away the underbrush that hides the winning idea—in any well-hidden stroke problem.

B—Now the basic theme is beginning to emerge.

C—This subtle 'slip' allows White to get into position for the compound stroke in the offing.

D—Triple Number One!

E—Triple Number Two!

F—Now into the basic First Position win.

Waste Not, Want Not

You waste valuable time if you fail to utilize the golden moments your adversary uses. You may actually be winning, or drawing the game then and there. (T.W.)

The Kings and I

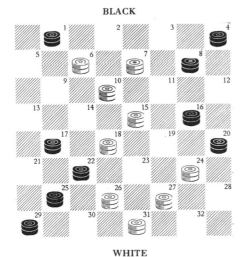

BLACK

WHITE

Problem No. 45
By Tom Wiswell
BLACK: kings 1, 4, 8, 16, 17, 20, 22, 25, 29
WHITE: kings 6, 7, 10, 15, 18, 24, 26, 27, 31
White to play and win

Solution

27-23—A, 20-27, 31-24—B, 22-31, 24-27, 31-24, 15-19!—C, 24-22, 23-18, 22-15—D, 10-3, 1-10, 7-30—E. White wins.

A—There are no variations in this 'Battle Royal'; all moves given are necessary—in the proper sequence.

B—Note how White gets the Black kings in position for the kill.

C—This double gambit is the move most solvers overlook; did you?

D—Now watch as the king on 10 doubles back to 3 to allow for the final flourish, a neat and useful maneuver.

E—Problems using only kings, may not be as practical as others, but they can be entertaining and even, at times, instructive.

Victory in Defeat

What is defeat? Nothing but education, nothing but the first step to something better. (Wendell Phillips)

In other words, defeat should make you better, not bitter. (T.W.)

Volcano

BLACK

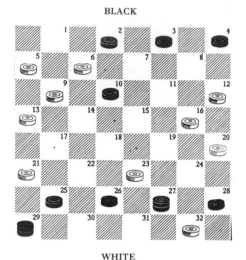

WHITE

Problem No. 46
By Tom Wiswell
BLACK: 2, 3, 4, 10, 25, 26, 28, kings
27, 29
WHITE: 5, 6, 9, 12, 13, 16, 20, 21,
23, 32
White to play and win

Solution

23-18, 27-23—A, 16-11—B, 23-14, 12-8, 3-12, 20-16, 12-19, 11-8, 4-11,
5-1, 14-5, 13-9, 5-14, 1-5, 2-9, 21-17—C, 14-21, 5-30, 21-17, 30-14—D.
White wins.

A—Of course, if 27-24, 6-1, 10-14 (otherwise 9-6), 18-15, 24-19, 15-10,
White wins.

B—The volcano starts to erupt!

C—The devastation is now complete.

D—Those who scoff at stroke problems as being just showy do not realize that
the mechanics and devices utilized therein can be helpful in ordinary
games—and enable the solver to exercise and enlarge his powers of concen-
tration and visualization. Yes, there is instruction as well as entertainment in
the serious study of problems of all types, including the scientific stroke.

Buried Alive

BLACK

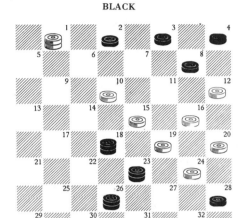

WHITE

Problem No. 47
By Tom Wiswell
BLACK: 2, 3, 4, 8, 28, kings 18, 23, 26
WHITE: 10, 12, 15, 16, 19, 20, 24, 32, king 1
White to play and win

Solution

15-11—A, 8-15, 32-27—A, 23-32, 10-7, 3-10—B, 12-8, 4-11, 16-7, 2-11, 20-16—C, 11-27, 1-6, 15-24, 6-31—D. White wins.

A—Watch how White proceeds to bury Black in the double corner.

B—Of course, 2-11, 16-7, 3-10, 12-8, etc. leads to the same dead-end.

C—Supplying the necessary waiting move to seal Black's doom.

D—A ghoulish finish that Edgar Allan Poe, an ardent devotee of Checkers, would have relished. The tricky endings of many stroke problems are comparable to the surprises sprung at the conclusion of good mystery yarns.

The Little Foolers

In the field of 2-against-2, and 3-against-3 problems alone there are situations that even top masters might not be sure of solving correctly in crossboard play! (J.L.)

End of a Perfect Play

BLACK

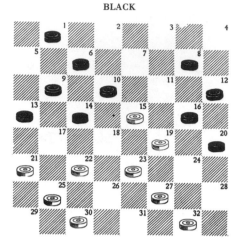

WHITE

Problem No. 48
By Tom Wiswell
BLACK: 1, 6, 8, 9, 10, 12, 13, 14, 16, 20
WHITE: 15, 19, 21, 22, 23, 25, 27, 30, 32
Black to play and draw

Solution

1-5—A, 22-18—B, 13-17—C, 30-26—D, 20-24!!!—E, 27-4, 12-16—F, 19-12, 10-19—F, 23-16, 14-30—F, 21-14, 30-21—G. Drawn.

A—Although Black is a man ahead his outlook appears bleak.

B—Necessary, as 32-28 and 30-26 permit 14-18.

C—Black's last move, but it is a good one, forcing 30-26.

D—Setting the stage for one of the most spectacular crossboard shots I've ever seen.

E—This took my worthy opponent completely by surprise, and also shocked a large gallery of spectators.

F—Now the fine details of the plot come into view.

G—This unusual draw enabled me to tie a ten game match with the noted Morris Krantz. Played in New York City more than thirty years ago.

Turning the Tables

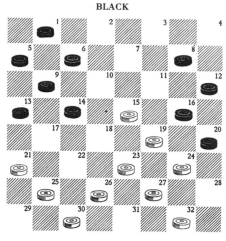

BLACK

WHITE

Problem No. 49
By Tom Wiswell
BLACK: 1, 5, 6, 8, 9, 12, 13, 14, 16, 20
WHITE: 15, 19, 21, 23, 24, 25, 26, 27, 30, 32
Black to play and win

Solution

6-10—A, 15-6, 1-10, 25-22, 8-11, 22-18—B, 13-17, 30-25—C, 17-22, 26-17, 9-13, 18-9, 13-29, 9-6, 10-14, 6-2, 29-25, 2-6—D, 25-22, 6-9 (6-1, 22-26), 14-18, 23-14, 16-23, 27-18, 20-27, 32-23, 22-15, 9-13, 11-16, 13-17, 15-18—E. Black wins.

A—This ending came up in a recent New York Tourney and my opponent, the popular Jimmy Ricca, playing White, thought he had a win. But soon he realized it *was* a win . . . for Black! It happens to all of us.

B—If 32-28, 11-15, 30-25, 14-18, 23-7, 16-30, 7-2, 30-26, 2-7, 26-17, 21-14, 9-18, 7-10, 13-17, 10-19, 17-21, 19-15, 21-30, 15-22, 12-16, 22-18, 30-26 (30-25, 18-23, draws), 18-23 (18-14, 26-22), 26-19, 24-15, 16-19, Black wins.

C—If 32-28, 17-22, 26-17, 9-13, 18-9, 5-14, Black wins.

D—If 2-7, 25-22, 7-3, 22-26, 21-17, 14-21, 32-28, 26-22, 3-8, 5-9, 8-15, 9-14, Black wins.

E—A tough one for White to lose after having such an apparently strong mid-game. But in Checkers looks can often be deceiving.

The Herd Laddie

BLACK

Problem No. 50
By James Wyllie
BLACK: 3, 6, 11, 12, 13, 14
WHITE: 19, 20, 21, 22, 23, 28
Black to play and draw

WHITE

Solution

13-17—A, 22-13, 3-7, 20-16, 11-20, 19-15, 12-16, 15-11, 7-10, 11-7, 10-15, 7-2, 6-10, 2-6, 15-19!—B, 6-24, 20-27, 28-24, 16-20, 24-19, 27-31, 19-16, 31-27, 23-19, 27-24, 19-15, 24-19—C. Drawn.

A—This position arises from a number of openings. For example: 9-14, 22-18, 5-9, 24-19, 11-15, 18-11, 8-24, 28-19, 4-8, 25-22, 8-11, 27-24, 11-15, 32-28, 7-11, 30-25, 1-5, 22-18, 15-22, 25-18, 9-13, 18-9, 5-14, 24-20, 2-7, 26-22, 14-17, 21-14, 10-26, 31-22, 7-10, 29-25, 10-14, 25-21. Forms diagram.

B—The key maneuver that saves the game for Black. Be on the lookout for this instructive ending as it can be reached via a number of routes.

C—James Wyllie (the 'Herd Laddie' from Scotland), one time world champion, vs. W. H. Broughton.

William F. Ryan

The late Willie Ryan, one of my earlier teachers and co-associates, was a great pioneer in Three-Move Play. His *Encyclopedia of Checkers* laid much of the groundwork in this. (T.W.)

29 Fifty Selected Games and 50 More Problems

The following section offers fifty critical positions arising from fifty separate games. As before, the solution to each problem position is shown beneath the diagram. Also, beneath each problem solution there is a move-by-move account of its generative game—up to the stage where the diagrammed position is formed.

So what you have here are not only fifty instructive Problems (as in the previous section) but also fifty instructive Games.

You may prefer first to direct your attention to all the Problems, or first to all the Games. But for a better sense of actual crossboard combat, it is recommended that you run up each game on your board, observe how the problem situation emerges, and then try to come to grips with it just as if you were the player.

Regardless of which approach you choose, you should gain much in instructive and entertaining rewards. You will see what sort of end-game or mid-game situations can evolve from a game, sometimes with an awareness of how the expert maneuvers toward creating a situation he desires. You will appreciate the neatness and beauty with which the expert resolves the problem situation, and will become alerted to the thematic ideas involved. And over all, you will gain a better sense of the general formational procedures as developed during the course of a game between experts.

The Three-Move Restriction style of play (see earlier chapter, "Just for Openers") prevails in professional checker circles; accordingly the games here are indexed by featuring the first three moves of each at the top of its page.

For your convenience in locating any Three-Move Opening game, the openings have been arranged in the conventional sequence through the fifty successive games. This sequence is based upon viewing the board from the

White side and regarding each opening move in turn from left-to-right order. So—first come the three-movers that begin with 9-13, then with 9-14, then 10-15, then 11-15, then 11-16, and finally 12-16. Under each, the sequence of White's reply is similarly from left to right: 21-17, 22-17, 22-18, 23-18, 23-19, 24-19, and 24-20.

There are 142 Three-Move Openers recognized as acceptable by the American Checker Federation; of course only a portion of these are represented in the fifty games that follow.

New Year's Resolution

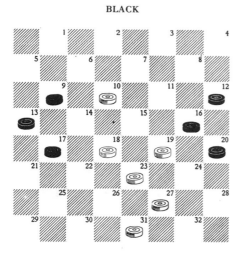

Problem No. 51
From Game Opening: 9-13, 22-18, 12-16
By Tom Wiswell
BLACK: 9, 12, 13, 16, 17, 20
WHITE: 10, 18, 19, 23, 27, 31
Black to play and win

Solution

17-22, 19-15 (10-6, 13-17), 13-17, 18-14, 9-18, 23-14, 16-19, 10-7, 17-21, 7-2, 21-25, 2-7, 25-30, 7-11—A, 12-16, 15-10—B, 30-25, 11-8—C, 22-26, 31-22, 25-9, 8-12, 9-14, 10-7, 14-18, 7-3, 18-22, 3-7, 22-26—D. Black wins.

A—If 14-9, 30-25, 15-11, 22-26, 31-22, 25-18, 7-10, 18-15, Black wins.

B—If 14-9, 30-25, 15-10, 22-26, 31-22, 25-18, 11-8, 19-24, Black wins.

C—11-15, 19-24, 15-18, 16-19, etc. Black wins.

D—From: 9-13, 22-18, 12-16, 24-20, 8-12, 27-24, 3-8, 24-19, (25-22 is best) 11-15, 18-11, 8-24, 20-11 (Or 28-19), 7-16, 28-19, 4-8, 26-22, 8-11, 22-18, 6-9, 25-22, 16-20, 30-26, 11-16, 32-27, 1-6!, 18-15, 13-17!, 21-7, (22-13, 10-14) 2-25, 29-22, 6-10, 22-18, 9-13, 26-22, 5-9, 18-15? (27-24 draws), 10-14, 15-10, 14-17, 22-18, forms diagram. Winning this game against Jack Botte enabled me to take first money in a New York Knockout Tourney on New Year's Day, 1974.

The Pin

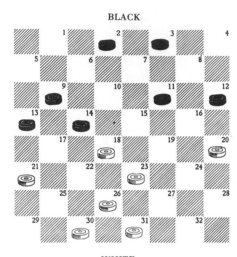

Problem No. 52
From Game Opening: 9-13, 24-20, 5-9
By Tom Wiswell
BLACK: 2, 3, 9, 11, 12, 13, 14
WHITE: 18, 20, 21, 23, 26, 30, 31
White to play and win

Solution

31-27—A, 3-7, 27-24, 7-10—B, 24-19, 13-17—C, 20-16!—D, 11-20, 19-16, 12-19, 23-16, 14-23, 21-7, 2-11, 26-19—E. White wins.

A—Compare with Problem No. 90, page 118, 'Science of Checkers', by Wiswell.

B—If 11-16, 20-11, 7-16, 24-20, 16-19, 23-16, 12-19, 26-23, 19-26, 30-23, White wins.

C—Desperate situations call for desperate measures.

D—The theme referred to in note A. The win was missed in a recent game at the New York Club . . . it can arise from many openings.

E—The pin is mightier than the sword! From: 9-13, 24-20, 5-9, 22-18, 10-14, 25-22, 6-10, 27-24, 1-5, 24-19, 11-15, 18-11, 8-24, 28-19, 14-17, 21-14, 9-27, 32-23, 4-8, 22-18, 8-1, 29-25, 5-9? (10-14 draws), 25-21, 10-15, 19-10, 7-14. Forms diagram.

Delight in a Challenge

The real mark of the creative person is that the unforeseen problem is a joy and not a curse. (Norman H. Mackworth)

Crossboard Levitation

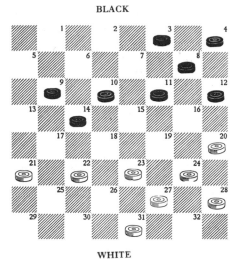

WHITE

Problem No. 53
From Game Opening: 9-13, 24-20, 5-9
Leo Levitt vs. Dr. Marion F. Tinsley
BLACK: 3, 4, 8, 9, 10, 11, 12, 14
WHITE: 20, 21, 22, 23, 24, 27, 28, 31
Black to play and draw

Solution

11-15—A, 24-19, 15-24, 28-19, 8-11, 20-16—B, 11-20, 22-18—B, 4-8, 18-15, 12-16!, 15-6, 8-12, 19-15, 16-19, 23-16, 12-19, 6-1, 19-23, 27-18, 14-23, 1-6, 9-14, 6-10, 14-18, 10-14, 3-8, 15-10, 8-12, 10-7, 12-16, 7-3, 20-24, 3-7, 16-20, 7-11, 24-27, 31-24, 20-27, 11-15, 18-22, 14-18, 22-26, 18-22, 27-31, 15-18—C. Drawn.

A—White's position is strong and Black must navigate with care.

B—A fine gambit on the part of White and typical of Dr. Tinsley's style of play in making the most of any given situation.

C—From: 9-13, 24-20, 5-9, 22-18, 10-14, 25-22, 6-10, 28-24, 10-15, 22-17, 13-22, 26-10, 7-14, 30-26, 15-22, 26-10, 2-7, 10-6, 1-10, 29-25 (21-17, 10-14), 10-14 (10-15, 21-17, 9-13, 17-14, 7-10, 14-7, 3-10, 25-21, 12-16, 32-28, 8-12, 24-19, 15-24, 28-19, 4-8, 27-24, 10-14. Drawn), 25-22, 7-10, 32-28. Forms diagram. Mr. Levitt is California Champion and rates as one of America's top masters.

Timely Arrival

BLACK

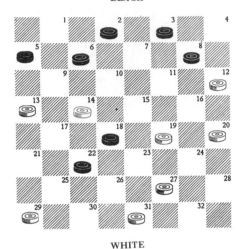

WHITE

Problem No. 54
From Game Opening: 9-14, 22-17, 5-9
By Tom Wiswell
BLACK: 2, 3, 5, 6, 8, 18, 22
WHITE: 12, 13, 14, 19, 20, 27, 29, 31
Black to play and draw

Solution

2-7—A, 19-15, 22-25, 29-22, 18-25, 20-16, 25-30, 16-11, 7-16, 27-23, 30-25, 23-18, 6-10!, 15-6, 25-22 (8-11 loses), 14-10, 22-15, 13-9—B, 5-14, 6-2, 15-6, 2-18, 16-19 (necessary), 18-15, 19-24, 31-26, 24-28, 26-23, 28-32, 23-18, 32-27, 18-14, 27-24, 14-9, 24-20, 9-6, 20-16, 6-2, 16-11, 15-10, 11-16, 2-7, 16-20, 10-6, 3-10, 6-15, 8-11, 15-8, 20-16. The Black king has arrived in time to hold two with one!—C. Drawn.
A—A drawing position that had been questioned in the past.
B—If 6-1, 15-6, 1-10, 8-11, etc. draws.
C—From: 9-14, 22-17, 5-9, 17-13, 1-5, 24-19, 11-16, 25-22, 14-17, 21-14, 9-25, 30-21, 10-14, 26-22, 7-10, 28-24! (22-17 is usual) 16-20, 22-17, 8-11, 19-15, 11-18, 23-19, 12-16, 19-12, 18-22, 24-19, 20-24, 27-20, 14-18, 32-27, 4-8, 17-14, 10-17, 21-14. Forms diagram.

Who Gives a Dama?

In most cases it is better to sacrifice your opponent's checkers rather than your own. (T.W.)

Safe and Sound

BLACK

WHITE

Problem No. 55
From Game Opening: 9-14, 22-17, 11-16
By Tom Wiswell
BLACK: 2, 5, 7, 10, king 25
WHITE: 8, 13, 14, 17, 28
White to play and draw

Solution

28-24—A, 25-22, 24-20—A, 2-6—B, 20-16, 22-18, 16-11, 7-16, 14-7, 18-15—C, 7-3, 15-11, 8-4, 16-19, 3-8, 11-7, 8-12, 19-23, 4-8, 7-2 (7-10, 8-11), 8-11, 23-26, 12-16, 26-30, 16-19, 30-25, 19-15, 25-21, 17-14—D. Drawn.

A—White goes to square 20, prepared to go 20-16, when necessary, and it is hard to see how Black can score.

B—If 22-26, (22-18, 8-3, etc. draws) 8-3, 26-23, 3-8, 23-19, 8-12, 2-6, 20-16, 10-15, 16-11, 7-16, 14-10, draws.

C—If 16-19, 17-14, 18-9, 7-2, etc. draws.

D—From: 9-14, 22-17, 11-16, 24-19, 8-11, 25-22, 11-15, 17-13, 15-24, 28-19, 4-8, 22-18, 8-11, 18-9, 5-14, 29-25, 16-20, 19-16, 12-19, 23-16, 10-15, 25-22, 14-18, 30-25, 1-5, 21-17, 6-10, 26-23, 3-8, 23-14, 8-12, 32-28, 12-19, 22-18 (*Not* 13-9, 20-24, 27-20, 11-16. Black wins. Stephen Fairchild vs. Arthur Reisman), 15-29, 27-24, 20-27, 31-8, 29-25. Forms diagram.

Strickland's Draw

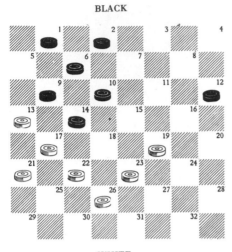

Problem No. 56
From Game Opening: 9-14, 22-17,
11-16
By W. Strickland
BLACK: 1, 2, 6, 9, 10, 12, 14
WHITE: 13, 17, 19, 21, 22, 23, 26
Black to play and draw

Solution

10-15—A, 19-10, 6-15, 17-10, 9-14, 13-9—B, 12-16, 9-5, 16-20, 22-17,
2-6—C, 26-22, 14-18—C, 23-14, 6-9—D. Drawn.

A—This beautiful drawing theme arises from various openings and, therefore,
should be studied by every student—and expert.

B—If 22-17, 15-18—BB, 23-19, 18-23, 26-22, 23-26, 13-9, 26-30, 17-13,
30-25, 22-17, 25-22, 19-15, 22-18, drawn.

BB—If 2-6, 26-22, 12-16, 23-18, 14-23, 17-14, 15-19, 10-7, 6-10, 21-17,
10-15, 7-3, 19-24, 3-7, 15-19, etc., drawn—N. H. Rubin vs. Guy Garwood.

C—Now into the climax of the drawing idea.

D—Here is just one run-up: 9-14, 22-17, 11-16, 24-19, 8-11, 25-22, 11-15,
17-13, 15-24, 28-19, 4-8, 29-25, 8-11, 22-17 (If 22-18, 10-15!, Black can
obtain a winning Dyke formation), 11-15, 25-22, 15-24, 27-11, 7-16, 23-19,
16-23, 26-19, 3-8, 30-26, 8-11, 26-23, 5-9, 32-28, 11-15, 31-26, 15-24,
28-19. Forms diagram.

Originality

Originality is simply a fresh pair of eyes. (Woodrow Wilson)

BLACK

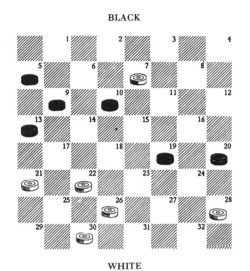

WHITE

Problem No. 57
From Game Opening: 9-14, 22-18, 11-15
By J. Robertson and P. Rule
BLACK: 5, 9, 10, 13, 19, 20
WHITE: 7, 21, 22, 26, 28, 30
White to play and win

Solution

26-23—A, 19-26, 30-23, 10-15—B, 23-19, 15-24, 28-19, 20-24, 7-2, 24-27, 2-7, 27-31, 7-10, 31-27, (31-26, 10-15) 19-16, 27-23, 16-11, 23-19, 11-7, 19-23, 7-3—C, 23-19, 3-8, 19-23, 8-12, 23-19, 10-7, 19-23, 7-11, 9-14, (23-19, 11-16) 12-16, 23-26, 11-7, 26-17, 7-10, 14-18, 21-14, 13-17, (18-23, 10-15) 16-19, 18-22, (17-21, 14-9) 10-6, 22-25, 6-9, 25-30, 9-13, 17-22, 19-23, 22-25, 13-17, 25-29, 17-21—D. An "American Position" ending! White wins.

A—If 7-3, 10-14, 3-7, 14-17, 21-14, 9-25, 30-21, 20-24, etc. Drawn
B—Threatening 15-18; If 10-14, 22-18, 13-17, 7-2, etc. White wins.
C—7-2 is wasting time, this is to the point of the matter.
D—From: 9-14, 22-18, 11-15, 18-11, 8-15, 25-22, 6-9, (5-9 is best) 29-25, 9-13, 23-18, 14-23, 27-11, 7-16, 22-18, 4-8, 18-15, 10-19, 24-15, 3-7, 25-22, 1-6, 28-24, 16-19, 32-28, 12-16, 24-20, 8-12, 20-11, 7-16, 31-27, 2-7, 15-11, 7-10, 27-23, 6-9, 11-7, 16-20, 23-16, 12-19. Forms diagram.

Hellman's Escape

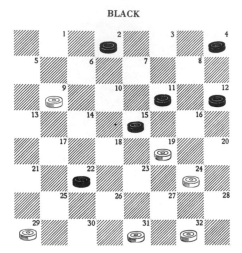

WHITE

Problem No. 58
From Game Opening 9-14, 22-18, 11-16
By Walter Hellman
BLACK: 2, 4, 11, 12, 15, 22
WHITE: 9, 19, 24, 29, 31, 32
Black to play and draw

Solution

15-18—A, 24-20, 18-23, 9-5, 23-26, 5-1, 26-30, 1-5, 2-6—B, 5-1, 6-10, 32-28, 30-26, 1-6, 26-23—C, 6-8, 4-11, 28-24, 23-16, 31-27, 22-26, 29-25, 26-31, 25-21, 31-26, 21-17, 26-22, 17-13, 11-15—D, 20-11, 15-18, 11-7, 12-16, 24-20, 16-19, 20-16, 22-26—E. Drawn.

A—This position had been considered a loss until the late Mr. Hellman played it in his successful 1967 Three-Move World Title Match with Gene Frazier.

B—The star move that saves the entire line of play.

C—Continuing the process of salvaging this pretty variation.

D—Playing to the gallery, of course, as 22-18, 13-9, 18-15, 27-23, 15-10, etc. also draws.

E—From: 9-14, 22-18, 11-16, 18-9, 5-14, 23-19, 16-23, 27-9, 6-13, 24-19, 8-11, 26-23, 11-15, 28-24, 1-6, 30-26, 7-11, 26-22, 6-9, 22-18, 15-22, 25-18, 12-16, 19-12, 10-15, 21-17, 13-22, 12-8, 3-12, 23-19, 9-14 (better than 9-13), 18-9. Forms diagram.

Never Say Die

Now and then, good players may resign, but they never give up! (T.W.)

126

Salvation

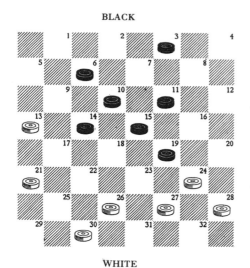

BLACK

WHITE

Problem No. 59
From Game Opening 9-14, 22-18, 11-16
By Tom Wiswell and W. F. Ryan
BLACK: 3, 6, 10, 11, 14, 15, 19
WHITE: 13, 21, 24, 26, 27, 28, 30
Black to play and draw

Solution

11-16—A. 24-20, 14-18—B, 20-11, 19-23—B, 26-19, 15-31, 11-7, 31-26!—C, 30-14, 10-17, 21-14, 3-17—D. Drawn.

A—If 3-7, 30-25, 14-18, 26-22, 10-14, 24-20, 6-10, 13-9, 14-17, 22-13, and either 19-24 or 18-23 leaves Black dangling.

B—Once thought to be a White win, but Black has a saving maneuver at the very last moment.

C—The key to Black's salvation and the idea that was evidently overlooked by the early Three-move analysts.

D—From: 9-14, 22-18, 11-16, 18-9, 5-14, 25-22 (best), 16-19, 24-15, 10-19, 23-16, 12-19, 22-17, 6-10, 27-24, 2-6, 24-15, 10-19, 17-10, 7-14, 29-25, 8-11, 25-22, 11-15, 22-17, 6-10, 17-13, 1-6, 32-27, 4-8, 27-24, 8-11, 31-27. Forms diagram. A basic formation from several openings.

The Right Approach

The Checker student should not so much learn "how to win" as "how not to lose." (T.W.)

Straitjacket

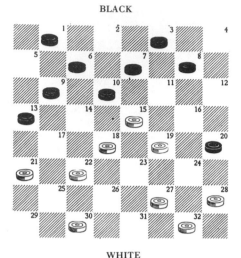

Problem No. 60

From Game Opening 9-14, 23-18, 14-23

By Tom Wiswell

BLACK: 1, 3, 6, 7, 8, 9, 10, 13, 20

WHITE: 15, 18, 19, 21, 22, 27, 28, 30, 32

Black to play and win

Solution

8-12, 30-26 (What else?), 10-14, 26-23 (27-23, 7-10), 13-17—A, 22-13, 3-8, 28-24, 7-11, 32-28—B, 11-16—C. Black wins.

A—Giving up a piece to put White in a straitjacket from which he cannot escape. (This move can be transposed with 3-8 which comes next.)

B—If 7-10, 32-28, 1-5, 21-17, 14-21, 18-14, etc. Draws.

D—This game won a New York Knockout for me in the finals with New Jersey expert Ted Reed (March 3, 1973). The game: 9-14, 23-18, 14-23, 27-18, 5-9, 26-23, 11-15, 18-11, 8-15, 22-18, 15-22, 25-18, 12-16, 24-19, 16-20, 29-25, 4-8, 25-22, 9-13, 31-27 (30-26 was expected and is better), 6-9, 18-15?, 2-6, 23-18. Forms diagram.

It Takes Two to Tango!

Before you concoct your plan, decoct your opponent's—or yours may be knocked into a cocked hat! (J.L.)

Escape Route

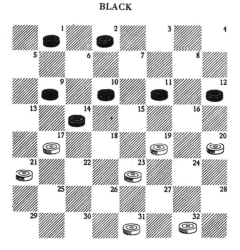

BLACK

WHITE

Problem No. 61

From Game Opening 9-14, 23-19, 5-9

Tom Wiswell vs. Howard Peck

BLACK: 1, 2, 9, 10, 11, 12, 14

WHITE: 17, 19, 20, 21, 23, 31, 32

White to play and draw

Solution

17-13, 2-7, 13-6, 14-18, 23-14, 10-17, 21-14, 1-17, 32-27—A, 17-22—B, 27-23, 7-10, 23-18, 22-25, 31-26, 25-30, 26-22, 30-25 (30-26 no better), 22-17, 25-21, etc.—C. Drawn.

A—If 31-27, 7-10, 27-24, 11-15, 32-28, 17-22, 20-16, 22-26, 16-11, 26-31, 11-7, 31-27, etc. Black wins.

B—Because White is threatening 19-16, etc.

C—From: 9-14, 23-19, 5-9, 27-23, 11-15, 22-18, 15-22, 25-18, 7-11 (best), 19-15 (26-22 is good), 10-19, 23-7, 14-23, 26-19, 3-10, 29-25, 8-11, 25-22, 4-8, 30-26, 11-15, 26-23, 9-14, 24-20, 15-24, 28-19, 8-11, 22-17, 6-9. Forms diagram.

Honest, Abe?

You can beat some of the players all of the time, and all of the players some of the time, but you cannot beat all of the players all of the time. (T.W.)

Billy's Goat

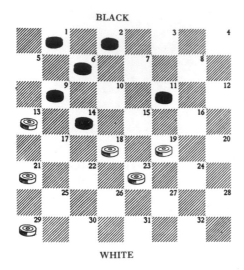

BLACK

WHITE

Problem No. 62

From Game Opening 9-14, 23-19, 11-16

Jules Leopold vs. Billy Hannigan

BLACK: 1, 2, 6, 9, 11, 14

WHITE: 13, 18, 19, 21, 23, 29

Black to play and draw

Solution

6-10—A (the only one!), 13-6, 2-9, 29-25, 9-13!, 18-9, 11-15, 19-16, 10-14, 16-11, 15-18, 23-19, 13-17, 10-7, 17-22, 7-2, 22-29, 2-7, 29-25—B. Drawn. Note also that if White now continues with 7-10, he loses by 25-30, 10-17, 18-22, 17-26, 30-16, 21-17, 16-11, 17-14, 11-7, 9-5, 1-6!, 5-1, 6-9, 14-5, 7-10.

A—*Not* 11-15, 18-11, 1-5, because then White puts the kibosh on Black's game by 11-7, 2-11, 21-17, 14-21, 23-18, White wins. In the game with Billy Hannigan, I (Jules Leopold) had some moves earlier planned for making this 11-15 pitch. When I got here I should have looked again (advice I give others!). I didn't, and Billy was quick to take advantage . . . breaking my streak of consecutive wins in our session.

Upon post-mortem examination I found the above draw. Later, Abe Bernstein advised me that the great Willie Ryan, in another opening, lost in exactly the same way to Mike Lieber. Of course, Ryan later found the same draw.

B—From: 9-14, 23-19, 11-16, 27-23, 16-20, 32-27, 5-9, 22-17, 8-11, 19-16, 12-19, 24-8, 4-11, 26-22, 11-15, 22-18, 15-22, 25-18, 7-11, 17-13, 11-16, 28-24, 16-19, 24-15, 10-26, 30-23, 3-8, 27-24, 20-27, 31-24, 8-11, 24-19. Forms diagram.

Double Cornered

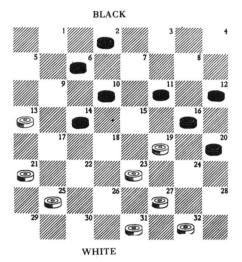

Problem No. 63
From Game Opening 9-14, 24-19,
11-15
By James Ferrie
BLACK: 2, 6, 10, 11, 12, 14, 16, 20
WHITE: 13, 19, 21, 23, 25, 27, 31,
32
White to play and win

Solution

25-22, 11-15, 22-17, 15-24, 23-19, 16-23, 27-9, 12-16, 9-5, 16-19, 32-28, 10-15, 5-1, 6-10, 13-9, 19-23, 28-19, 15-24, 1-6, 10-15, 6-10, 15-19, 10-15, 23-27, 9-5, 27-32, 5-1, 32-28, 17-14, 19-23, 15-19, 23-27, 21-17—A, 27-32, 1-6!, 2-18, 19-23, 18-27, 17-13—B. White wins.

A—The quiet before the storm. Just when it appears that Black has survived, White lowers the boom

B—From a 'Double Corner Opening' game between J. Moir and J. Ferrie. 9-14, 24-19, 11-15, 28-24, 5-9, 22-18, 15-22, 25-18, 8-11, 24-20, 11-16, 20-11, 7-16, 18-15, 3-7, 15-11, 1-5, 26-22, 9-13, 22-18, 16-20, 18-9, 7-16, 29-25, 5-14, 25-22, 13-17, 22-13, 4-8, 30-25, 8-11 (loses. 2-7 draws narrowly—James Searight). Forms diagram.

One Hundred and One

It may take a hundred moves to win a game but it takes only one move to lose it. (T.W.)

Mantell's Escape

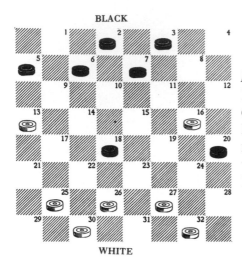

BLACK

WHITE

Problem No. 64
From Game Opening 10-14, 22-18, 6-10
By A. J. Mantell
BLACK: 2, 3, 5, 6, 7, 18, 20
WHITE: 13, 16, 25, 26, 27, 30, 32
Black to play and draw

Solution

6-10—A, 26-23, 10-14, 32-28, 2-6—B, 16-12, 6-10—C, 13-9, 3-8!—D, 12-3, 14-17—D, 23-14, 17-22—D, 25-18, 10-17, 3-10, 5-32—E. Drawn.

A—White appears strong but Black has a plan for survival.

B—Watch every move closely, the fireworks are coming.

C—Letting White through—but that's all part of the plan.

D—A beautiful drawing device originated by the late great analyst, A. J. Mantell. He was probably the author of more new three-move play than any other analyst in his day.

E—From: 10-14, 22-18, 6-10, 25-22, 12-16, 22-17 (the 24-20, 16-19 drawable gambit forms the "White Doctor" opening), 16-20, 17-13, 1-6, 29-25, 11-15, 18-11, 8-15, 24-19, 15-24, 28-19, 4-8, 19-15, 10-19, 23-16, 8-12, 27-23, 12-19, 23-16, 14-17, 21-14, 9-18, 31-27. Forms diagram.

Foolproof

Having blind faith in a "foolproof" system may only be proof that one is a blind fool. (Dr. Arnold Gallub)

Sidestep

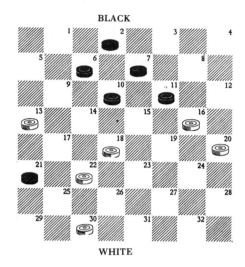

Problem No. 65.

From Game Opening 10-14, 22-18, 11-15

Samuel Gonotsky vs. Mike Lieber

BLACK: 2, 6, 7, 10, 11, 21

WHITE: 13, 16, 18, 20, 22, 30

Black to play and draw

Solution

6-9, 13-6, 2-9, 16-12, 10-14, 12-8, 14-23, 8-3, 7-10, 3-7, 10-15, 7-16, 15-19, 16-11, 19-24, 11-15, 23-27, 15-18, 9-13—A, 20-16, 27-31, 16-11, 24-27, 11-7, 27-32, 7-2, 32-27, 2-7, 27-23, 18-27, 31-24, etc.—B. Drawn.

A—This must be played now, else White would hold the two men to the side of the board and win. Back in 1928, Samuel Gonotsky, the former United States Champion, played this ending against the great Mike Lieber in their titanic struggle which ended in forty draws.

B—From: 10-14, 22-18, 11-15, 18-11, 8-15, 26-22, 6-10, 22-17, 4-8, 23-19, 8-11, 17-13, 1-6, 25-22, 14-17, 21-14, 9-25, 29-22, 5-9, 27-23, 9-14, 31-26, 14-17, 24-20, 15-24, 28-19, 11-15, 32-28, 15-24, 28-19, 7-11, 22-18, 3-7, 19-16, 12-19, 23-16, 17-21, 26-22. Forms diagram.

So It Seems!

In Checkers, between the opening and the ending there is . . . the muddle game. (T.W.)

American Escapade

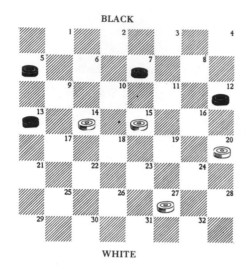

Problem No. 66

From Game Opening 10-14, 22-18, 12-16

Jimmy Ricca vs. Tom Wiswell

BLACK: 5, 7, 12, 13

WHITE: 14, 15, 20, 27

Black to play and draw

Solution

13-17, 27-23, 17-22, 23-18—A, 22-26, 15-10, 26-31—B, 10-3, 31-26, 18-15—C, 26-22, 3-7, 22-18, 15-11, 18-9, 7-10, 9-13, 11-7, 5-9, 7-2, 13-17, 2-6, 9-13, 6-9, 17-21, 9-14, 13-17, 10-15, 17-22, 20-16, 12-19, 15-24, 22-25, 24-27, 25-29, 27-23, 21-25 (avoiding the "American Position" loss), 23-26, 25-30—D. Drawn.

A—If 23-19, 22-26, 20-16, 26-31, 15-11, 31-27, 11-2, 27-24, drawn.

B—If 7-11, 10-7, 26-31, 7-3, 31-26, 3-8, etc. White wins.

C—14-10, 26-22, 18-15, 22-18, 15-11, 18-15, 10-6, 15-8, 6-2, 5-9 (or 8-11), 2-6, 9-13, 6-10, 8-11, 10-14, 11-8!, 14-18, 8-11, 18-22, 11-8, etc. Drawn-Gus Pilarsky vs. Tom Wiswell.

D—From: 10-14, 22-18, 12-16, 24-20, 16-19, 23-16, 14-23, 26-19 (a drawable gambit), 8-12, 31-26, 6-10, 25-22, 11-15, 27-23, 15-24, 28-19, 4-8, 22-17, 9-13, 17-14, 10-17, 21-14, 1-6, 29-25, 6-10, 25-21, 10-17, 21-14, 2-6, 23-18, 8-11!, 19-15 (anything better?), 12-19, 15-8, 3-12, 18-15, 6-9 (Or 13-17), 32-27, 9-18, 26-23, 19-26, 30-14. Forms above diagram.

Fred Allen's Win

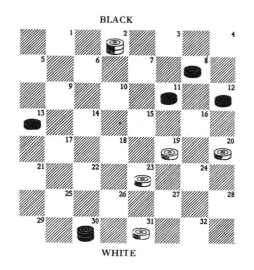

BLACK

WHITE

Problem No. 67
From Game Opening 10-14, 23-19,
14-18
By Fred Allen
BLACK: 8, 11, 12, 13, king 30
WHITE: 19, 20, 23, 31, king 2
White to play and win

Solution

31-26 (if 2-7, 11-15 draws), 13-17, 2-6, 17-21, 6-9, 21-25, 9-14, 25-29,
14-17, 29-25, 17-21, 25-29, 26-22, 29-25 (if 30-26, 23-18), 23-18, 25-29,
18-15!—A, 11-25, 19-15—B. White wins.

A—The beautiful climax to Mr. Allen's famous win. The late Fred Allen was a
star of yesteryear (before the Fred Allen of radio fame), and his games and
problems are remembered for their practicality as well as their beauty.

B—The "Allen Win" can come up in many ways. Here is just one illustration:
10-14, 23-19, 14-18, 22-15, 11-18, 21-17, 9-13, 26-22, 7-11, 22-15, 11-18,
17-14, 8-11, 24-20, 3-7, 19-15, 4-8, 25-21, 13-17—C, 30-25, 6-10, 15-6,
1-10, 28-24, 11-15, 31-26, 2-6, 25-22, 18-25, 29-13, 10-17, 21-14, 6-10,
13-9, 10-17, 9-6, 7-11, 27-23, 17-21, 32-28, 21-25 24-19, 15-24, 28-19,
25-30, 6-2, 5-9, 2-6, 9-13 (if 9-14, 6-2, then 14-17—as 14-18 loses right
away!), 6-2. Forms diagram after first move of solution.

C—Loses; Nathan Rubin vs. Edwin Hunt, 1934. And 18-22 loses by 14-9.
Instead, 6-10, 15-6, 1-17, 21-14, 11-15, etc. will draw—W. F. Ryan.

A Checker Mnemonic

Forget your losses, but remember *why* you lost. (J.L.)

Case Against the Defense

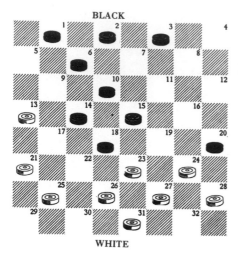

BLACK

WHITE

Problem No. 68
From Game Opening 10-14, 24-20,
14-18
By Basil Case
BLACK: 1, 2, 3, 6, 10, 14, 15, 18, 20
WHITE: 13, 21, 23, 24, 25, 26, 27,
28, 31
White to play and win

Solution

26-22—A, 3-8, 24-19—A, 15-24, 28-19, 20-24—B, 27-20, 18-27, 31-24, 8-12—C, 22-17, 14-18, 17-14, 10-17, 21-14, 18-23, 14-10, 6-15, 19-10, 23-26, 24-19, 26-30, 25-22!—D, 30-25, 22-18, 25-22, 19-15, etc.—E. White wins.

A—This bind on the Black pieces ultimately proves fatal.

B—This defense, by the late L. M. Lewis, puts up a strong resistance—but runs out of steam at a critical juncture.

C—The Black game looks solid enough, but it's only a surface appearance.

D—*Not* 25-21 which only draws. This is the key to the White win.

E—A fine win by the former American Champion from Alabama. Mr. Case is the author of that fine work *My Best Checkers*. From: 10-14, 24-20, 14-18, 22-15, 11-18, 23-14, 9-18, 21-17, 12-16? (8-11 draws), 20-11, 8-15, 17-13, 5-9, 25-21, 9-14, 29-25, 4-8, 28-24, 8-11, 26-23, 11-16, 32-28, 16-20, 30-26, 7-10. Forms diagram.

Counterpunch

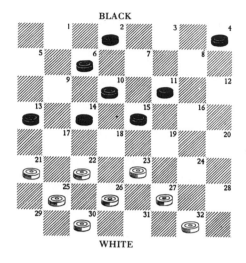

BLACK

WHITE

Problem No. 69
From Game Opening 10-14, 24-20, 11-16
By George King
BLACK: 2, 4, 6, 10, 11, 13, 14, 15
WHITE: 21, 22, 23, 25, 26, 27, 30, 32
White to play and win

Solution

23-18, 14-23, 27-18, 6-9—A, 21-17, 4-8, 32-28—B, 8-12, 28-24, 11-16—C, 18-11, 10-15 (nice try, but . . .), 11-7!, 2-11, 24-20, 16-19, 26-23, 19-26, 30-23, 12-16, 25-21, 15-19, 23-18—D. White wins.
A—Because otherwise 18-14, 10-17, 21-14, White wins.
B—if 32-27, 10-14, 17-10, 13-17, 22-6, 15-31, etc. Drawn.
C—If 12-16, 24-20, 16-19, 26-23, etc., White wins.
D—From: 10-14, 24-20, 11-16, 20-11, 8-15, 28-24, 6-10, 24-20, 1-6, 22-18, 15-22, 25-18, 3-8, 26-22, 9-13, 18-9, 5-14, 31-26, 12-16, 20-11, 8-15, 29-25, 7-11 (loses. 6-9 draws). Forms diagram.

Unfinished Anthology

M. Francis Tescheleit spent an entire lifetime working on *Master Play of the Draughts Board* yet never brought it to completion. (T.W.)

Crocodile

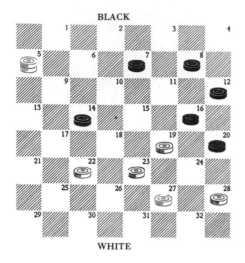

BLACK

WHITE

Problem No. 70

From Game Opening 10-15, 21-17, 9-13

By Richard Fortman

BLACK: 7, 8, 12, 14, 16, 20

WHITE: 19, 22, 23, 27, 28, king 5

White to play and win

Solution

5-9, 14-18, 22-15, 7-11, 9-14, 11-18, 19-15, 18-22, 14-17, 22-26, 17-22, 26-31, 22-17, 31-24, 28-19, 20-24—A, 23-18, 16-23, 15-11—B. White wins.

A—The famous "Crocodile Position" by Captain Fishburne can arise from 9-13, 22-17, 13-22, 25-18, 11-16, 29-25, 5-9, 18-14, 9-18, 23-14, 10-17, 21-14, 8-11, 24-19, 16-23, 26-19, 6-10, 25-21, 10-17, 21-14, 11-16, 28-24, 16-23, 27-18, 7-11, 30-26, 11-16, 26-23, 16-20, 31-27, 2-7, 24-19, 7-11, 14-10, 11-16, 18-15, 4-8 (1-5 draws), 10-6, 1-10, 15-6, 3-7, 6-2, 7-10, 2-6, 10-14, 6-10, 14-17, 10-14, 17-22, 14-17, 22-26, 32-28, 26-31, 19-15, 31-24, 28-19, 20-24, and the tail snaps again.

B—From: 10-15, 21-17, 9-13, 17-14, 11-16, 23-19, 16-23, 26-10, 6-15, 27-23, 8-11, 32-27, 4-8, 22-18, 15-22, 25-18, 11-16, 29-25, 8-11, 25-21, 16-20, 24-19, 11-16, 30-25, 1-6, 14-9, 5-14, 18-9, 13-17, 21-14, 6-13, 14-9, 13-17 25-22, 17-26, 31-22, 7-10, 9-5, 10-14, 5-1, 3-8, 1-5, 2-7—C. Forms diagram.

C—Loses. Instead 2-6, 22-18, 6-10, 18-9, 8-11, 9-6, 10-14, 19-15, 11-18, 28-24, 18-22, 5-9, 14-17, 9-14, 17-21, 14-17, 22-26, 17-22, 26-31, 23-18, 16-19, draws—Walter Hellman vs. Richard Fortman.

Rare Gift

BLACK

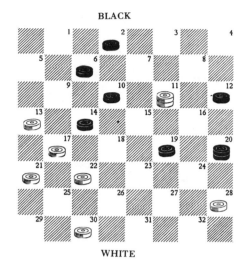

WHITE

Problem No. 71

From Game Opening: 10-15, 21-17, 6-10

Billy Hannigan vs. Tom Wiswell

BLACK: 2, 6, 10, 12, 14, 19, king 20
WHITE: 13, 17, 21, 22, 28, 30, king 11

Black to play and draw

Solution

20-24—A, 11-16—B, 2-7, 16-23, 24-19, 23-16, 12-19, 22-18—C, 14-23, 17-14, 10-17, 21-14, 6-10, 14-9, 7-11, 9-6, 11-16, 6-2, 23-26, 30-23, 19-26—D. Drawn.

A—Beware of 14-18, 22-15, 19-23, 17-14!, 10-19, 14-10. White wins.

B—White has nothing better.

C—Best. If 30-26, 7-11, 28-24, 19-28, 26-23, 11-15, 22-18, 15-22, 23-19, drawn.

D—From a short match played on November 9, 1973. The ability to spot such saving sacrifices may seem to be a rare gift, but it can be acquired through study and experience. Game: 10-15, 21-17, 6-10, 17-14, 9-18, 23-14, 10-17, 22-13, 11-16, 25-22, 8-11, 29-25, 4-8, 24-20, 16-19, 27-24, 1-6, 25-21, 5-9, 22-17, 7-10, 32-27, 9-14, 27-23, 3-7, 23-16, 12-19, 31-27, 8-12, 27-23, 11-16, 20-11, 7-16, 24-20, 15-18, 20-11, 18-27, 11-8, 27-31, 26-22, 31-27, 7-3, 27-24!, 3-8, 24-20!, 8-11. Forms diagram.

Wrap-Up

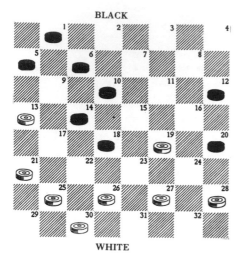

BLACK

WHITE

Problem No. 72
From Game Opening: 10-15, 21-17, 15-18
By August Heffner
BLACK: 1, 5, 6, 10, 12, 14, 18, 20
WHITE: 13, 19, 21, 25, 26, 27, 28, 30
White to play and win

Solution

28-24, 10-15, 19-10, 6-15, 13-9—A, 12-16, 9-6!—B, 1-10, 26-23, 5-9, 30-26, 9-13, 26-22—C. White wins.

A—Right into the enemy territory. Not always a good idea, you must judge each situation with care.

B—Why it was a good idea in this case: White places Black in a straitjacket from which he cannot extricate himself. If 26-23 instead, Black gets out by 16-19, 23-16, 15-19, 24-15, 18-22, drawn.

C—Wiswell won this from Morris Krantz many years ago, but Mr. Heffner first scored the same win: 10-15, 21-17, 15-18, 22-15, 11-18, 23-14, 9-18, 24-19, 8-11, 17-13, 7-10, 25-21, 10-14, 29-25, 4-8, 26-23, 11-16, 28-24, 16-20, 31-26, 2-7, 32-28, 8-11, 19-16, 12-19, 24-8, 3-12, 23-19, 7-10 (7-11 draws, this loses). Forms diagram.

Don't Overextend

The win is often the enemy of the draw. (J.L.)

Lucas Denied

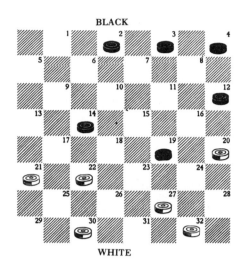

BLACK

WHITE

Problem No. 73
From Game Opening: 10-15, 21-17, 15-18
By Tom Wiswell
BLACK: 2, 3, 4, 12, 14, 19
WHITE: 20, 21, 22, 27, 30, 32
Black to play and draw

Solution

3-8—A, 27-23—B, 19-26, 30-23, 2-6, 32-28, 12-16, 20-11, 8-15, 22-17, 6-10, 17-13, 4-8 (best), 28-24, (13-9, 8-11) 8-11, 23-19, 15-18, 13-9, 18-23, 9-6, 23-27, 6-2, 27-32, 24-20—C, 11-15, etc.—D. Drawn.

A—If 4-8, 27-23, 19-26, 30-23, 2-6, 22-18, 6-9, 32-28, 8-11, 28-24, 3-7, 24-19, 7-10, 20-16 (A winning sacrifice; the "Lucas Position." Observe!), 11-20, 18-15, 20-24, 15-6, 24-27, 6-1, 27-31, 1-6, 31-27, 6-13, 27-18, 13-9, White wins—Harold Freyer

B—If 20-16, 14-18, 22-15, 8-11, etc. draws.

C—If 2-6, 11-16, 6-15, 16-23, 24-20, 23-26, etc. draws.

D—From 10-15, 21-17, 15-18, 22-15, 11-18, 23-14, 9-18, 25-21, 8-11, 29-25, 5-9, 17-13, 9-14, 24-20, 11-15, 28-24, 7-10, 26-23, 15-19, 24-15, 10-26, 31-15, 6-9, 13-6, 1-19, 25-22. Forms diagram.

Develop Slowly

Moves that disturb your position the least—disturb your opponent the most! (T.W.)

Quinlan's Quirk

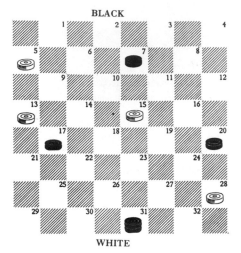

BLACK

WHITE

Problem No. 74
From Game Opening: 10-15, 21-17,
11-16
By Tom Quinlan
BLACK: 7, 17, 20, king 31
WHITE: 5, 13, 15, 28
White to play and draw

Solution

5-1, 31-26—A, 1-6, 26-23, 6-9!—B, 23-18, 9-14, 18-11, 14-21, etc.—C.
Drawn.

A—31-27, 28-24, 27-23, 15-11. Drawn. The same theme saves White in this
classic problem: Black on 7, 20, king 32. White on 15, 22, 28. White to move
and draw. 22-17 is necessary. Then, 32-27, 28-24, 27-23 and . . . what is
White's only move to draw?

B—If 6-2, 17-22, 2-11, 20-24, etc., Black wins.

C—From: 10-15, 21-17, 11-16, 22-18, 15-22, 25-18, 8-11, 17-13, 16-20,
29-25, 9-14, 18-9, 5-14, 24-19, 11-16, 19-15, 4-8, 23-19, 16-23, 27-9,
7-10, 25-22, 10-19, 22-18, 3-7, 32-27, 12-16, 9-5, 8-12, 27-23, 20-24,
30-25 (*not* 26-22, 19-26, 30-23, 24-27, 31-24, 16-20), 7-10, 25-22—D,
16-20, 23-16, 12-19, 22-17, 24-27, 31-15, 10-19, 18-15, 2-7, 26-22 (or
17-14), 18-23, 22-18, 23-26, 17-14, 6-10, 15-6, 1-17, 18-15, 26-31. Forms
diagram.

D—25-21, 24-27, 31-15, 10-19, 18-15, 16-20, 23-16, 12-19, 15-11, 20-24,
26-23, 19-26, 28-19, 26-31, 11-8, 31-27, 8-4, 27-23, 19-16, 23-19, 16-12,
19-16, 4-8, 6-10, 8-3, 10-14, etc. Drawn—Mike Lieber.

Abdication

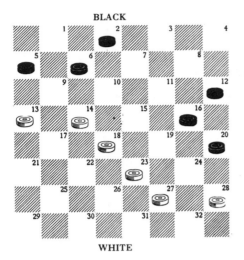

Problem No. 75
From Game Opening: 10-15, 21-17,
11-16
By Billy Hannigan and Tom Wiswell
BLACK: 2, 5, 6, 12, 16, 20
WHITE: 13, 14, 18, 23, 27, 28
White to play and draw

Solution

28-24—A, 6-9, 13-6, 2-9, 14-10, 9-13—B, 10-6, 13-17—B, 6-2, 17-22—B, 2-6—C, 22-26, 6-9!—D, 5-14, 18-9, 26-31, 23-18, 31-26, 18-14, 26-22, 9-6, 22-18, 14-10—E. Drawn.

A—If 14-9 (18-15, 16-19), 5-14, 18-9, 6-10, 23-18, 2-7, 9-6, 7-11, 6-2, 10-15, 18-14, 15-19, etc. Black wins.

B—Black has his eye on some of those White pieces that appear vulnerable. How does White save them? That is today's lesson.

C—If 2-7, 22-26, 7-11, 26-31, 18-14, 31-26, 24-19, 26-31, 27-24, 20-27, 11-20, 27-32, 23-18, 32-27, 19-15, 31-26, 15-11, 26-22, 18-15, 27-23, 14-10, 22-18, 10-6, 18-14! etc. Black wins.

D—Giving up the newly crowned king. But abdicating the throne saves the game!

E—From: 10-15, 21-17, 11-16, 17-14, 9-18, 23-14, 8-11, 25-21, 6-9, 29-25, 9-18, 24-19, 15-24, 22-8, 4-11, 28-19, 16-23, 27-18, 12-16, 21-17, 16-19, 17-14, 1-6, 31-27, 11-16, 32-28, 16-20, 25-21, 7-11, 21-17, 11-16, 17-13, 3-8, 26-23, 19-26, 30-23, 8-12. Forms diagram—Billy Hannigan vs. Tom Wiswell. Mr. Hannigan won the 1973 Major Tourney at Lakeside, Ohio, and this game was played shortly afterward.

Ward's Way

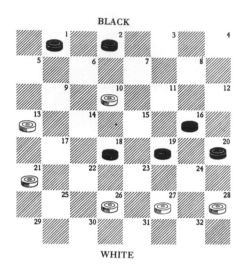

BLACK

WHITE

Problem No. 76
From Game Opening: 10-15, 22-17,
11-16
By R. T. Ward
BLACK: 1, 2, 16, 18, 19, 20
WHITE: 10, 13, 21, 26, 27, 28
White to play and win

Solution

13-9—A, 1-5, 10-6—A, 5-14, 6-1, 2-6 (anything better?), 1-17, 18-22,
17-14, 22-31, 14-10, 31-24, 10-15—B. White wins.

A—With these moves White fashions a brilliant win.

B—From the Kelso opening: 10-15, 22-17, 11-16, 24-19, 15-24, 28-19,
9-14, 17-10, 6-24, 27-11, 8-15, 23-18, 15-22, 25-18, 12-16, 29-25, 16-19,
18-14, 7-11, 25-22, 11-15, 21-17, 4-8, 30-25, 8-12, 25-21, 12-16, 17-13,
16-20, 32-28, 3-8, 22-17, 8-12, 31-27, 15-18 (2-6, 26-22, 5-9, 14-5, 6-10,
13-9, 19-24, etc. Drawn) 14-9, 5-14, 17-10, 12-16—Ċ. Forms diagram.

C—Loses 2-6—D, 10-7, 1-5, 7-3, 6-10, 3-7, 10-15, 7-2, 18-22, 26-17,
15-18, draws—J. Alexander.

D—1-5 is also a neat win for White: 1-5, 10-6, 2-9, 13-6, 5-9, 6-1, 9-13,
1-6, 18-22, 26-17, 13-22, 6-10, 22-26, 10-15, 19-24, 28-19, 26-31, 27-23,
31-27, 15-18, 27-24, 19-15, 12-16, 21-17, 24-19, 18-22, 19-10, 22-18.
White wins. A classic theme, watch for it in your games.

Highland Fling

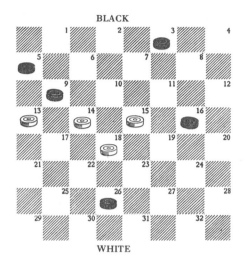

BLACK

WHITE

Problem No. 77
From Game Opening: 10-15, 22-18, 15-22
By Richard Jordan
BLACK: 3, 5, 9, 16, 26
WHITE: 13, 14, 15, 18
Black to play and win

Solution

26-30—A, 13-6, 30-26, 6-2, 16-20, 2-6, 26-22, 14-10, 20-24, 6-2, 22-26, 15-11, 26-23, 18-15, 23-18, 2-6, 24-27, 6-1, 18-14 (or 27-31, and if 10-6, then 3-7!), 11-7, 14-18, 15-11, 18-15—B. Black wins.

A—Although Richard Jordan defeated Robert Stewart in this game Mr. Stewart won the heat by two wins to one with nine draws. The event was the First ScottishTourney in 1893. Although three players who held the world title at one time (Jordan, Stewart and Ferric) were entered, the two finalists were W. Bryden and A. Jackson. Mr. Bryden emerged the winner in this star-studded event. However, it was a "sudden-death" tourney; the loss of a single heat meant elimination.

B—From: 10-15, 22-18, 15-22, 25-18, 11-16, 29-25, 16-20, 24-19, 8-11, 18-14, 9-18, 23-14, 11-16, 25-22, 16-23, 26-19, 4-8, 22-18, 6-9, 30-26, 1-6, 26-23, 6-10, 18-15, 10-17, 21-14, 9-18, 23-14, 7-11, 15-10, 11-15, 27-23, 15-24, 28-19, 8-11, 23-18, 11-16, 19-15, 16-19, 31-26, 20-24, 26-22, 12-16, 22-17, 24-27, 32-23, 19-26, 10-6 (loses. 15-11, 26-30, 10-7, 3-10, 14-7, 30-26, 7-3, 16-20, 18-15, 26-22, 17-13, 22-18, 15-10, draws), 2-9, 17-13. Forms diagram.

Nice Try

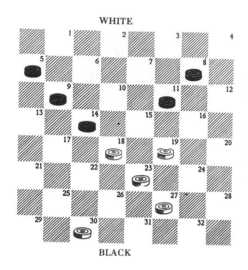

WHITE

BLACK

Problem No. 78

From Game Opening: 10-15, 22-18, 15-22

By Tom Wiswell

BLACK: 5, 8, 9, 11, 14

WHITE: 18, 19, 23, 27, 30

White to play and win

Solution

27-24—A, 9-13—B, 18-9, 5-14, 24-20, 13-17 (8-12, 30-26), 30-26, 11-15—C, 19-10, 8-11, 10-6, 11-15, 6-2, 15-18, 23-19, 18-23, 2-6—D, 23-30, 6-9, 14-18, 9-14—E. White wins.

A—This came from a game that I won from Billy Hannigan, in a New York Knockout Tourney, August 3, 1973.

B—If 8-12, 24-20, 9-13, 18-9, 5-14, 30-26, etc., White wins.

C—Nice try, but it just falls short.

D—Gaining the man, the game, the heat and the tourney!

E—From: 10-15, 22-18, 15-22, 25-18, 6-10, 18-14, 9-18, 23-14, 10-17, 21-14, 12-16, 29-25, 11-15 (1-6 is good), 24-19, 16-23, 26-10, 2-6, 27-23, 6-15, 23-19, 15-24, 28-19, 1-6, 25-22, 8-11, 31-26, 6-9, 22-18, 7-10, 14-7, 3-10, 32-27, 10-14, 26-23, 4-8 (loses. 9-13 or 14-17 draws). Forms diagram.

Poker Face

Take a lesson from the poker player—if you see you have a losing position don't tip off your opponent by facial expression or gesture. (T.W.)

Man on First

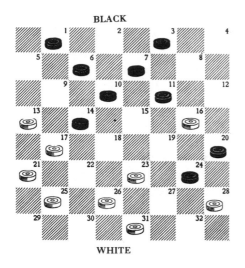

BLACK

WHITE

Problem No. 79
From Game Opening: 10-15, 23-18, 9-14
By Dr. Marion Tinsley
BLACK: 1, 3, 6, 7, 10, 11, 14, 20, 24
WHITE: 13, 16, 17, 21, 23, 25, 26, 28, 31
Black to play and win

Solution

11-15, 28-19, 15-24, 25-22, 10-15, 17-10, 7-14, 22-18, 15-22, 26-10, 6-15, 23-19, 15-18, 19-15, 24-28—A, 15-10, 28-32, 16-11, 18-22, 11-7, 20-24, 7-2, 32-27, 2-6, 27-23, 6-9—B, 22-25, 9-14, 25-29, 21-17—B, 29-25, 10-7, 3-10, 14-7, 1-6!, 7-11, 23-18, etc.—C. Black wins.

A—Black spent considerable time here, possibly checking to see that White did not have a pitch-out to break the ensuing Bridge. It is also well within the realm of possibility that the final, climactic move was visualized at this stage. (Richard Fortman)

B—White, of course, wants to break that Bridge.

C—From: 10-15, 23-18, 9-14, 18-9, 5-14, 22-17, 7-10, 26-23, 11-16, 24-19, 15-24, 28-19, 8-11, 25-22, 16-20, 30-26, 11-15, 19-16? (32-28 is safe), 12-19, 23-16, 15-19, 29-25, 4-8, 17-13, 2-7, 22-17, 8-11, 27-23, 19-24, 32-28. Forms diagram—Dr. Marion Tinsley vs. Ed Scheidt.

Following the Numbers Is Not Enough

Many master the arithmetic of Checkers . . . but few the algebra. (T.W.)

Golden Opportunity

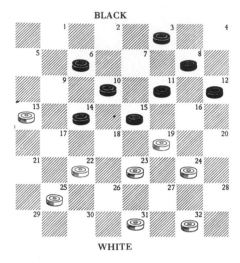

Problem No. 80
From Game Opening: 10-15, 23-18, 6-10

Dr. Marion Tinsley vs. Derek Oldbury

BLACK: 3, 6, 8, 10, 11, 12, 14, 15
WHITE: 13, 19, 22, 23, 24, 25, 31, 32

White to play and win

Solution

13-9!—A, 6-13, 25-21, 3-7—B, 31-26—C, 13-17—D, 22-13, 15-18, 13-9, 18-27, 32-23, 14-17, 21-14, 10-17, 24-20, 17-21, 9-6, 21-25, 6-2, 25-30 (25-29, 20-16), 19-16—E, 12-19, 23-16, 30-23, 16-12—F. White wins.

A—A beautiful pitch that wins nicely for White.

B—If 13-17, 22-13, 15-18, 24-20, 18-27, 31-24, etc. White can win.

C—In the 1974 National Tourney Derek Oldbury, against Dr. Marion Tinsley, allowed a draw by 32-28, 14-18, 23-14, 10-26, 19-3, 26-30, 3-7, 11-16, 7-10, 8-11, 24-20, 16-19, 31-27, 30-25, 10-14, 11-15, etc. Drawn.

D—If 11-16, 24-20, 15-24, 20-2, 10-15, 2-6, etc., White wins.

E—Necessary, as 20-16, 11-20, 2-4, 20-24, etc., only draws.

F—From: 10-15, 23-18, 6-10, 18-14, 9-18, 24-19, 15-24, 22-6, 1-10, 28-19, 11-15, 27-24, 8-11, 25-22, 11-16, 21-17, 16-23, 26-19, 5-9, 17-13, 2-6, 29-25, 9-14, 30-26, 4-8, 26-23, 7-11? (loses; 12-16, etc. best). Forms diagram. The crucial win was later pointed out by Leopold and other observers.

Derek Oldbury of Devon, England, is the official world's Go-As-You-Please champion. He defeated Elbert Lowder of Sanford, N.C. in a special match held August 1979 in Dublin for the GAYP title left open by Tom Wiswell's retirement. Mr. Oldbury is also an original and informative writer; his latest publication is *The Complete Encyclopedia of Checkers*.

A Snitch in Time

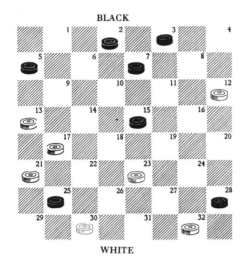

BLACK

WHITE

Problem No. 81

From Game Opening 10-15, 23-18, 6-10

By Tom Wiswell and Jimmy Ricca

BLACK: 2, 3, 5, 7, 15, 25, 28

WHITE: 12, 13, 17, 21, 23, 30, 32

Black to play and win

Solution

2-6, 17-14—A, 25-29, 21-17, 6-10—B, 32-27!, (hoping for 28-32, then 30-25), 15-18, 23-19, 28-32, 27-24, 32-27, 24-20, 27-31!, 19-16, 31-26!, 30-23, 18-27, 16-11 (13-9, 29-25), 7-16, 14-7, 3-10, 20-11, 29-25—D. Black wins.

A—If 30-26, 25-30, 26-22, 7-11, 23-18, 30-25, Black wins.

D—15-18, 23-19, 18-23—C, 19-16, 23 26 (23-27, 32-23, 28-32, 23-19, 32 27, 19-15, 7-10, etc. draws), 30-23, 29-25, 23-19, 25-22, 19-15, 7-10, 14-7, 3-19, 16-11, 22-18 (or 19-23), 12-8, 19-23, 8-3, 23-26, 3-7, 26-30, 17-14, (now or later), 18-9, 7-2, 30-26, 11-8, 26-23, 8-3, 23-18, 3-7, 18-15, now 7-3 draws. But the inviting 7-10 is a disaster!—by 15-11, 10-1, 11-15, 13-6, 15-11.

C—If 6-10, 19-16, 10-15 (18-23, 13-9), 32-27 (13-9 probably draws also), 28-32, 27-24, 32-27, 24-20, etc., drawn.

D—From: 10-15, 23-18, 6-10, 18-14, 9-18, 24-19, 15-24, 22-6, 1-10, 27-20 (28-19 is usual), 11-16, 20-11, 8-15, 28-24, 12-16, 24-20, 16-19, 21-17, 4-8, 17-13, 8-11, 25-21. 19-23, 26-19, 15-24, 21-17, 11-15, 29-25, 15-18, 25-21, 10-15, 31-26? (20-16 appears in order), 24-28, 20-16, 18-22, 26-23, 22-25, 16-12. Forms diagram.

The Old Switcheroo

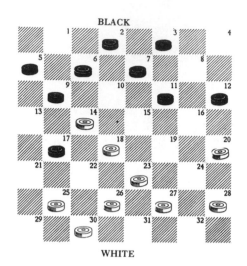

BLACK

WHITE

Problem No. 82
From Game Opening 11-15, 21-17, 9-13

By M. Martus and W. Hartzell

BLACK: 2, 3, 5, 6, 7, 9, 11, 12, 17

WHITE: 14, 18, 20, 23, 25, 26, 27, 28, 30

White to play and draw

Solution

28-24—A, 6-10—B, 26-22—C, 17-26, 25-22—C, 10-17, 22-6, 2-9, 18-15!—D, 11-18, 23-14, 9-18, 30-14, 7-10, 14-7, 3-10—E. Drawn.

A—The White game looks precarious, but the situation is well under control. In Checkers, surface appearances are often deceptive.

B—Black has nothing better at this point.

C—The start of an instructive combination that brings the game to a pleasing climax.

D—The key to the situation; a game to remember.

E—From: 11-15, 21-17, 9-13 (the 'Switcher' opening), 25-21, 8-11, 24-19, 15-24, 28-19, 11-15, 17-14, 15-24, 27-20, 10-17, 21-14, 4-8, 29-25, 6-9, 22-18, 8-11, 31-27, 13-17, 32-28, 1-6. Forms diagram.

The Realist

An optimist always sees the win, the pessimist always sees the loss, the master always sees the draw. (T.W.)

BLACK

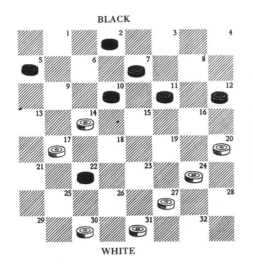

WHITE

Problem No. 83
From Game Opening 11-15, 21-17,
9-13
By James Wyllie
BLACK: 2, 5, 7, 10, 11, 12, 22
WHITE: 14, 17, 20, 24, 27, 30, 31
White to play and draw

Solution

27-23, 2-6, 23-18, 10-15—A, 17-13, 22-25—B, 30-21, 15-22, 24-19,
22-25, 31-26, 25-30, 26-23—C, 30-26, 23-18, 6-10, 13-9, 10-17, 21-14,
7-10—D, 14-7, 5-23, 7-3, 23-27, 3-8—E. Drawn.

A—12-16, 17-13, 10-17, 18-15, 11-18, 20-2, 18-23 (17-21, 2-9, 5-14,
13-9, 22-25, 9-6, 25-29, 6-2, 29-25, 2-6, 25-22, 6-9. White wins—James
Wyllie), 2-9, 5-14, 13-9, 23-27. Drawn.

B—6-10, 13-9, 10-17, 18-14, 7-10, 14-7, 5-14, 7-2, 12-16, 2-6, 14-18,
6-10, 16-19, 10-14, 19-28, 14-21, 22-25, 21-17, 25-29, 17-14, 18-23,
14-10, 15-19, 10-7, 11-15, 20-16, 28-32, 7-11, 15-18, 11-15, 32-28, 15-22,
23-26. Drawn.

C—26-22, 30-26, 22-18 draws same way, but if 21-17, 26-30, Black wins.

D—If 26-22, 19-15, 22-17, 15-8, 17-10, 18-15, 10-19, 8-3, drawn.

E—From: 11-15, 21-17, 9-13, 25-21, 8-11, 17-14, 10-17, 21-14, 6-10,
22-17, 13-22, 26-17, 15-18, 24-20, 3-8, 29-25, 1-6, 28-24, 18-22, 25-18,
11-16, 20-11, 8-22, 32-28, 4-8, 24-20, 6-9, 28-24, 9-18, 23-14, 8-11.
Forms diagram.

Double Jeopardy

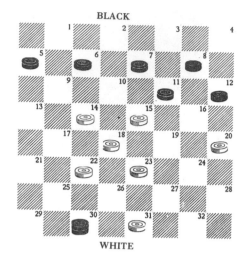

BLACK

WHITE

Problem No. 84
From Game Opening 11-15, 21-17, 9-13
By D. A. Brodie
BLACK: 5, 6, 7, 8, 11, 12, king 30
WHITE: 14, 15, 18, 20, 22, 23, 31
White to play and win

Solution

22-17, 30-25, 17-13, 6-10, 15-6, 25-22, 6-2, 22-15, 2-6, 12-16, 23-18—A, 15-22, 14-9—A, 5-14, 6-10 (Double jeopardy!), 16-19, 10-26, 11-15, 13-9, 7-10, 26-30, 15-18, 9-6, 18-22, 6-2, 10-14, 2-7, 14-17, 7-10, 19-24, 10-15, 17-21, 20-16, 8-12, 15-18 (30-26 will also win), 12-19, 18-25, 24-28, 25-22, 28-32, 22-26, 32-28, 31-27, 28-32, 27-24, 19-28, 26-23—B. White wins.

A—These moves lead to a fine problem finish by Mr. Brodie.

B—From: 11-15, 21-17, 9-13, 25-21, 8-11, 30-25, 4-8, 24-19, 15-24, 28-19, 11-15, 17-14, 15-24, 27-20, 10-17, 21-14, 8-11, 32-28, 6-10—C, 25-21, 10-17, 21-14, 1-6, 29-25, 6-10, 25-21, 10-17, 21-14, 2-6, 22-18, 13-17, 28-24, 17-21, 24-19, 21-25 (loses. 6-10 draws), 19-15, 3-8, 26-22, 25-30. Forms diagram.

C—12-16 (best), 22-17, 13-22, 25-18, 6-10, 29-25, 10-17, 25-21, 1-6, 21-14, 16-19, 23-16, 6-10, 28-24, 10-17, 26-22, 17-26, 31-22, 5-9, 24-19, 2-6, 22-17, 9-13, 17-14, 6-10, 16-12, 10-17, 12-8, 3-12, 19-15. Drawn—Robert Martins.

Backfire

The easiest way to lose is to try always to win. (T.W.)

Return Engagement

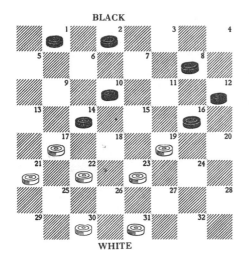

WHITE

Problem No. 85
From Game Opening 11-15, 21-17, 9-13
By Harry Jackson
BLACK: 1, 2, 8, 10, 12, 14, 16
WHITE: 17, 19, 21, 22, 23, 30, 31
White to play and draw

Solution

17-13, 8-11, 22-18, 1-5, 18-9, 5-14, 31-26—A, 2-7, 13-9, 11-15, 9-6, 15-24, 6-2, 7-11, 2-6, 11-15, 6-9, 15-18, 23-19, etc.—B. Drawn.

A—A fine move that leads to a draw arising from several openings, so it should be closely studied by the student.

B—From: 11-15, 21-17, 9-13, 25-21, 8-11, 24-19, 15-24, 28-19, 6-9 (troublesome), 22-18 (easier than 23 18 or 30-25), 13-22, 26-17, 9-14, 18-9, 5-14, 29-25, 11-15, 27-24, 4-8—C, 25-22, 8-11, 32-28, 11-16, 24-20, 15-24, 20-11, 7-16, 28-19, 3-8—E. Forms diagram.

C—15-18, 32-27, 7-11, 24-20, 3-8—D, 19-15, 10-26, 30-23, 1-5, 17-10, 18-22, Drawn—Jack Cox.

D—If 11-15, 30-26, 15-24, 20-16, 12-19, 27-20 draws. Or, if 4-8, 30-26, 11-15, 17-13, 15-24, 20-16, 12-19, 27-20, 18-27, 31-6, 1-10 draws.—Jack Cox. Both of these draws utilize the "Brooklyn stroke" idea.

E—16-20, 31-27, 3-8, 30-26, 8-11, 19-16, 12-19, 23-7, 2-11, 26-23, 11-16, 17-13, 10-15, 22-17, 15-19, 17-10, 19-26, 27-23, 26-31, 23-18. Drawn. J. Cox.

Into the Abyss

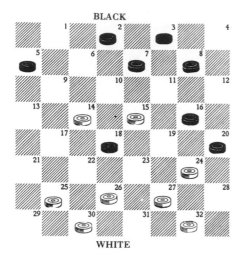

Problem No. 86

From Game Opening 11-15, 22-17, 15-18

By Tom Wiswell

BLACK: 2, 3, 5, 7, 8, 16, 18, 20

WHITE: 14, 15, 24, 25, 26, 27, 30, 32

White to play and win

Solution

15-10—A, 8-11—B, 26-23, 11-15—C, 23-19—D, 16-23, 10-6—D, 2-9, 25-22—D, 18-25, 27-2, 20-27, 30-21—E, 9-18, 32-14—F. White wins.

A—A forceful move, leaving Black very little choice.

B—If 7-11 (Or 8-12), 26-23, followed by 25-22, White wins.

C—Into the abyss, but there is nothing else.

D—These moves bring the game to a pleasing climax . . . and are more expeditious than 30-26.

E—The jump that hurts. From a New York Tourney, won by the writer on July 18, 1973.

F—From: 11-15, 22-17, 15-18, 23-14, 9-18, 17-14, 10-17, 21-14, 8-11, 24-19, 4-8, 28-24, 11-16, 26-23, 16-20, 31-26, 6-10? (6-9 safer), 25-21, 10-17, 23-14, 1-6, 29-25, 6-9, 19-15, 9-18, 21-14, 12-16, (if 2-6, 24-19). Forms diagram.

The Big Squeeze

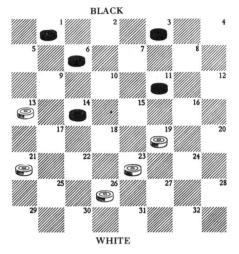

BLACK

WHITE

Problem No. 87

From Game Opening 11-15, 22-17, 15-19

Tom Wiswell vs. Jack Botte

BLACK: 1, 3, 6, 11, 14

WHITE: 13, 19, 21, 23, 26

Black to play, White draws

Solution

6-9—A, 13-6, 1-10, 26-22, 11-15, 19-16, 3-7, 21-17—B, 14-21, 23-18—C, 15-19, 18-15—C, 10-14, 22-17—C, 14-18, 17-14—D. Drawn.

A—If 6-10, 13-9, 3-7, 26-22, 11-15, 9-6, 15-24, 6-2, etc. Drawn.

B—The key to White's draw; a theme that frequently arises in play.

C—The "Big Squeeze" is on and Black must make way for the steal.

D—From: 11-15, 22-17, 15-19, 24-15, 10-19, 23-16, 12-19, 25-22, 8-11, 27-24 (27-23 is routine), 4-8, 24-15, 11-25, 29-22, 7-10, 22-18, 9-14, 18-9, 6-22, 26-17, 5-9, 17-13, 2-6, 30-26, 8-11, 31-27, 9-14, 27-23, 10-15, 28-24, 15-18, 24-19, 18-27, 32-23. Forms diagram. From my ten-game match with New Jersey Champion Jack Botte, which favored yours truly: 2-0-8 (May 14, 1973).

Sure Sign

You can tell an expert from a beginner. The expert looks before he moves, the beginner moves before he looks. (J.L.)

Restoration

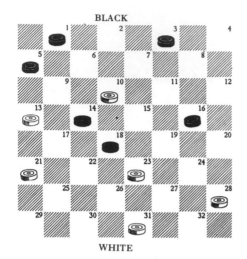

BLACK

WHITE

Problem No. 88
From Game Opening 11-15, 22-18,
15-22
By Harold Freyer and Tom Wiswell
BLACK: 1, 3, 5, 14, 16, 18
WHITE: 10, 13, 21, 23, 28, 31
White to play and draw

Solution

13-9—A, 18-27, 31-24, 16-20—B, 24-19, 14-18, 9-6, 18-23, 6-2, 23-26,
21-17—C, 26-31, 10-6, 1-10, 2-7, etc.—D. Drawn.

A—Improves on 31-27 as given by Ed Thompson in demonstrating a win for
the late Prof. W. R. Fraser against Tom Wiswell in their 1960 Free-Style
World Title match. (See *Art of Checkers*, Game One).

B—If 14-18, 24-20, 5-14, 20-11, 18-22, 11-7, 22-25, 7-2, 14-18, 2-6,
25-29, 6-9, 29-25, 9-14, 18-22, 28-24, 22-26, 14-18, 26-30, 24-20, 30-26,
20-16, 26-22, 18-23, etc. Drawn. (H. Freyer)

C—This idea, also the play in Note B, was evidently overlooked by Mr.
Thompson. These restore the draw to the Fraser-Wiswell game.

D—From: 11-15, 22-18, 15-22, 25-18, 8-11, 29-25, 4-8, 18-14, 9-18,
23-14, 10-17, 21-14, 11-15, 24-19, 15-24, 28-19, 8-11, 27-23, 11-15,
19-10, 6-15, 25-22, 12-16, 30-25, 7-11 (Mr. Thompson's move claimed to
correct 1-6 and to win), 25-21, 2-6, 32-28, 6-9, 14-10, 9-14, 22-18, 15-22,
26-17, 11-15, 17-13, 15-18. Forms diagram.

Sacrifice Hit

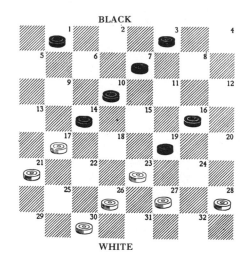

BLACK

WHITE

Problem No. 89
From Game Opening 11-15, 22-18, 15-22
By James Lees
BLACK: 1, 3, 7, 10, 14, 16, 19
WHITE: 17, 21, 23, 26, 27, 28, 30
White to play and win

Solution

27-24—A, 10-15, 17-10, 7-14, 21-17!—B, 14-21, 24-20, 1-6, 20-11, etc.—C. White wins.

A—The counterplay to a "logical-looking" but losing move in the Single Corner opening. Wiswell has won this with White in many an exhibition tour, yet ironically, it is Black who thinks he is going to win.

B—The scientific sacrifices that Black usually overlooks.

C—From: 11-15, 22-18, 15-22, 25-18, 8-11, 29-25, 4-8, 24-20, 10-15, 25-22, 15-19, 23-16, 12-19, 27-23, 8-12, 23-16, 12-19, 31-27, 9-14, 18-9, 5-14, 27-23, 11-16, 20-11, 7-16, 22-17, 6-10, 32-27 (setting the trap), 2-7 loses and forms diagram. But 3-8, 27-24, 2-6, 24-15, 10-19, 17-10, 6-15, 30-25, 1-6, 25-22, 6-10, 21-17, 8-12, 23-18, 19-23, etc. draws. (A. Bissett vs. C. Brown).

Triple Threat

Every true master is a "triple-threat" player—one who counts the study of the *end-game* as important as that of the *opening* and the *mid-game*. (T.W.)

Scot Free

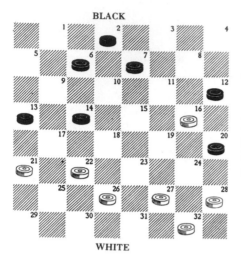

BLACK

WHITE

Problem No. 90
From Game Opening 11-15, 22-18, 15-22
By Willie Bryden
BLACK: 2, 6, 7, 12, 13, 14, 20
WHITE: 16, 21, 22, 26, 27, 28, 32
White to play and draw

Solution

16-11!—A, 7-16, 26-23, 16-19, 23-16, 12-19, 27-24, 20-27, 32-16, 2-7—B, 28-24, 6-10, 21-17!—C, 14-21, 22-18—C, 21-25, 24-19, 25-30, 18-15, 10-14, 15-10—D. Drawn.

A—If 27-23, 12-19, 23-16, 6-10, 16-12, 14-17, 21-14, 10-17, 12-8, 7-10, 22-18, 17-21, 28-24, 20-27, 32-23, 21-25, 18-15, 10-19, 23-16, 25-30, 26-23, 30-26, 23-19—AA, 26-23, 8-4, 13-17, 4-8, 17-21, 8-12, 23-27, 19-15, 27-24, 16-11, 24-19, 15-10, 19-15, Black wins. W. Bryden beat A. Jackson in the First Scottish Tourney finals in 1893, and Bryden went on to win the title.

AA—23-18, 26-23, 18-14, 2-6, 8-3, 13-17, 3-7, 23-18. Black wins.

B—Black expects to win with this move but all is not gold that glitters.

C—The instructive combination that saves the day for White.

D—From: 11-15, 22-18, 15-22, 25-18, 8-11, 29-25, 10-14, 24-19, 11-16, 27-24, 16-20, 31-27, 4-8, 25-22, 7-10, 30-25, 9-13, 18-9, 5-14, 22-18, 1-5, 18-9, 5-14, 25-22, 3-7, 19-16, 12-19, 24-15, 10-19, 23-16, 8-12. Forms diagram.

Two on the Side

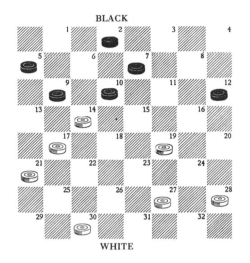

Problem No. 91

From Game Opening 11-15, 23-18, 12-16

By Tom Wiswell

BLACK: 2, 5, 7, 9, 10, 12

WHITE: 14, 17, 19, 21, 27, 28, 30

White to play and win

Solution

27-24, 9-18, 19-16, 12-19, 24-6, 2-9—A, 17-13, 9-14, 13-9, 18-23, 9-6, 23-27—B, 6-2, 7-11, 2-7, 11-16, 7-10, 14-18, 10-15, 18-22, 15-18, 22-25, 21-17, 25-29, 18-23, 27-32, 17-14, 16-20, 23-26!—C, 32-27, 28-24!—C, 27-23, 26-19, 20-27, 19-23, 27-32, 23-18, 32-27, 14-10, 27-24, 10-6, etc. eventually holding two Black pieces with one king.—D. White wins.

A—Forms an instructive end-game study for the student and expert.

B—Other moves can be tried but White wins with care.

C—These moves are expeditious and the win is soon evident.

D—From: 11-15, 23-18, 12-16, 18-11, 8-15, 24-20, 9-14, 20-11, 7-16, 22-18, 15-22, 25-9, 5-14, 26-23, 16-20, 29-25, 3-7? (4-8 is in order), 23-19, 4-8, 25-22, 8-12, 22-17, 14-18, 27-24, 20-27, 32-14, 1-5, 31-27, 6-9. Forms diagram. This game was won by the writer in a New York Knockout Tourney in 1973.

Daring Ideas

Daring ideas are like chessmen moved forward; they may be beaten, but they may start a winning game. (Goethe)

Lock-Up

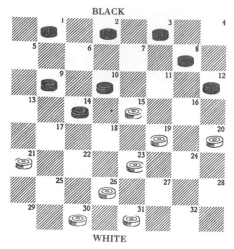

BLACK

WHITE

Problem No. 92

From Game Opening 11-15, 23-19, 9-14

By John Drummond

BLACK: 1, 2, 3, 8, 9, 10, 12, 14

WHITE: 15, 19, 20, 21, 23, 26, 30, 31

Black to Play and win

Solution

1-6—A, 26-22—B, 9-13, 30-25—C, 14-17, 21-7, 2-27, 31-24, 6-10, 22-18, 8-11, 25-21, 13-17!—D, 21-7, 3-10—E. Black wins.

A—This move effectively locks up the position and leads to an instructive win for Black.

B—If 20-16, 3-7, 16-11, 7-16, 26-22, 9-13, 22-18, 14-17, 21-7, 2-11, 30-25, 13-17, 25-21, 17-22, 21-17, 22-25, 17-14, 25-30, Black wins—J. Dent.

C—If 22-18, 3-7, 18-9, 13-17, 21-14, 6-13, 15-6, 2-27, 31-24, 7-10, Black wins.—John Drummond. An example of the "Brooklyn Stroke."

D—The key to the Black win. Although it leaves Black a man short, the positional advantage is enough to force White's resignation.

E—From: 11-15, 23-19, 9-14, 27-23, 8-11, 22-18, 15-22, 25-9, 5-14, 29-25, 11-15, 25-22, 7-11, 24-20, 15-24, 28-19, 11-15, 32-28, 15-24, 28-19, 6-9, 22-18, 4-8, 18-15, is diagrammed loss. Correct here is 20-16, then 2-7, 26-22, 8-11, 22-17, 11-20, 17-13, 1-6, 30-26, 20-24, 26-22, 24-28, 22-17, 28-32, 19-15. Drawn—A. Anderson.

Dunne In

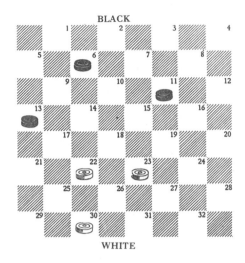

WHITE

Problem No. 93
From Game Opening 11-15, 24-19, 15-24
By Frank Dunne
BLACK: 6, 11, 13
WHITE: 22, 23, 30
White to play and win

Solution

23-19, 6-10—A, 22-18, 13-17, 30-26, 17-21, 26-22, 21-25, 18-15, 11-18, 22-6—B. White wins.

A—If 6-9, 30-25, 9-14, 25-21, White wins.

B—From: 11-15, 24-19, 15-24, 28-19, 9-14, 22-18, 5-9, 26-22, 8-11, 22-17, 9-13, 18-9, 13-22, 25-18, 6-13, 18-14, 10-17, 21-14, 11-16, 29-25, 4-8, 25-22, 7-10, 14-7, 3-10, 27-24, 16-20, 31-26, 20-27, 19-15, 10-19, 23-16, 12-19, 32-16, 8-11, 16-7, 2-11, 26-23, 1-6 (11-16 draws). Forms diagram.

Frank Dunne's theme can appear in several games. Now, knowing the idea, can you solve *this* little end-game problem?—Black on 3, 6, and 7. White on 12, 14, 15, and 30. White to move and win.

Idée Fixe

The play you do know can hurt you as much, if not more, than the play you don't know. (T.W.)

Timely Advice

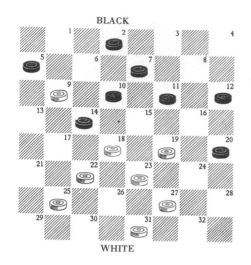

BLACK

WHITE

Problem No. 94

From Game Opening 11-16, 21-17, 16-20

By Harold Freyer and Tom Wiswell

BLACK: 2, 5, 7, 10, 11, 12, 14, 20

WHITE: 9, 18, 19, 22, 23, 25, 27, 31

Black to play and draw

Solution

11-15—A, 18-11, 7-16, 25-21 (22-18, 10-15), 14-18, 22-6, 5-14, 19-15, (31-26 is an easy draw), 2-9, 15-10, 9-13—B, 10-6, 13-17, 6-2 (31-26, 16-19, 23-16, 12-19, 6-2, 14-18 draws), 17-22, 2-6, 16-19—C, 23-16, 12-19, 6-10, 14-18, 10-14, 19-23, 27-24, 20-27, 31-24, 22-25—D. Drawn.

A—If 11-16, 25-21, 14-17, 22-13 (best), 5-14, 18-9, 7-11, 9-6, 2-9, 13-6, 11-15 (10-14, 21-17, 14-21, 6-2), 6-2, 15-24, 23-18, 24-28, 27-24, etc. White wins.

B—*Not* 16-19, 23-16, 12-19, 27-23, 19-26, 31-22, 20-24, 10-6, 24-27, 6-1, 27-31, 1-5, 9-13, 5-9. White wins.

C—Black has timed his moves correctly and is just in time to escape with a neat draw.

D—From: 11-16, 21-17, 16-20, 17-14, 10-17, 22-13, 9-14, 25-22, 8-11, 29-25, 11-15, 24-19, 15-24, 28-19, 6-10, 22-18, 4-8, 18-9, 5-14, 25-22, 8-11, 13-9, 11-15, 32-28 (better than 19-16), 15-24, 28-19, 3-8, 22-18, 8-11, 26-22, 1-5, 30-25. Forms diagram.

Backstop

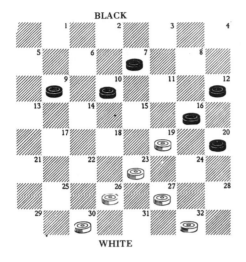

BLACK

WHITE

Problem No. 95

From Game Opening 11-16, 22-18, 16-20

By Tom Wiswell

BLACK: 7, 9, 10, 12, 16, 20

WHITE: 19, 23, 26, 27, 30, 32

White to play and win

Solution

23-18—A, 16-23, 26-19, 10-14—B, 19-15, 14-23, 27-18, 20-24, 30-26, 12-16, 26-22, 16-19, 22-17, 9-13, 17-14, 19-23, 14-9, 24-27, 18-14, 27-31, 9-6, 31-26, 6-2!—C. White wins.

A—The start of an instructive timing win by White.

B—Other moves may be made but to no avail, as you may verify.

C—Black's only waiting move is 13-17 and that backs up the Black man on 14, thereby spoiling the shot. I have won this from several opponents: 11-16, 22-18, 16-20, 18-14, 9-18, 23-14, 10-17, 21-14, 8-11, 25-22, 6-10, 29-25, 10-17, 22-13, 11-15, 24-19, 15-24, 28-19, 4-8, 25-22, 8-11, 22-18, 11-16, 26-23, 7-10, 18-15, 3-7, 15-6, 1-10, 31-26, 5-9 (loses. 7-11 draws), 13-6, 2-9. Forms diagram.

Excuses, Excuses

Don't make excuses when you lose. Your friends don't need them, and your enemies won't believe them. (J.L.)

Overdrawn

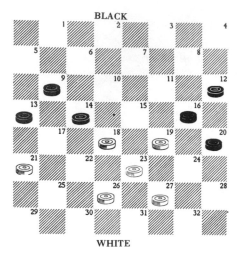

BLACK

WHITE

Problem No. 96
From Game Opening 11-16, 23-18, 7-11
By Tom Wiswell
BLACK: 9, 12, 13, 14, 16, 20
WHITE: 18, 19, 21, 23, 26, 27
Black to play and win

Solution

13-17, 19-15—A, 16-19, 23-16, 14-30, 21-5, 12-19, 15-10—B, 30-25, 5-1, 25-22, 1-6, 22-18, 6-9, 19-24—C. Black wins.

A—If 18-15, 9-13, 15-11, 14-18, 21-14, 13-17, etc., Black wins.

B—Because if 5-1, 30-26, 27-23, 19-24, etc., Black wins.

C—From: 11-16, 23-18, 7-11, 26-23, 3-7, 24-19, 11-15, 18-11, 8-24, 28-19, 4-8, 22-18, 8-11, 30-26 (25-22 usual), 9-14, 18-9, 5-14, 26-22, 16-20, 22-18, 1-5, 18-9, 5-14, 25-22, 11-15, 32-28, 15-24, 28-19, 7-11, 22-18, 11-16, 18-9, 6-13, 29-25, 2-6 (Black is fishing for a win!), 25-22, 6-9, 22-18, 10-14, 31-26 loses and forms diagram. 18-15, in place of 31-26, draws. However, with the strong side, White often dislikes allowing a quick, easy draw, then later finds he has dangerously overdrawn his play! The idea is a classical theme, and I have won with it on a number of occasions.

Played Out?

To those who say Checkers has become exhausted I reply: Only Checker *players* become exhausted. (T.W.)

Surprised Party

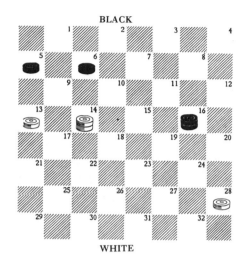

Problem No. 97
From Game Opening 11-16, 24-19,
8-11
By "The Pioneer"
BLACK: 5, 6, king 16
WHITE: 13, 28, king 14
White to play and win

Solution

28-24—A, 16-11—B, 24-19, 11-7, 19-15—C, 7-2, 13-9—D, 6-13, 15-
10—E. White wins.

A—The situation may look 'drawish' but White has "the move" and, as
frequently happens in the end-game, that is decisive.

B—Black feels perfectly safe as he heads for square 2 and an apparently easy
draw. If 16-20, 24-19, 20-24, 19-15, 24-19, 14-10, White wins.

C White can pitch now (13-9) but holds out till the bitter end.

D—This is a basic situation that arises from many games. The neat sacrifice
often comes as a stunning surprise to the party on the losing end.

E—From: 11-16, 24-19, 8-11, 22-17, 11-15, 17-13, 15-24, 28-19, 9-14,
25-22, 4-8, 22-18, 8-11, 18-9, 5-14, 29-25, 16-20, 25-22, 11-16, 22-18,
14-17, 21-14, 10-17, 18-14, 7-10, 14-7, 3-10, 23-18, 16-23, 26-19, 17-22,
32-28, 2-7, 18-15, 1-5, 27-24, 20-27, 31-24, 22-26, 30-23, 12-16, 19-12,
10-26, 12-8, 26-31, 8-3, 7-10, 24-19, 31-27, 3-7, 27-23? (10-14 Draws),
7-14, 23-16. Forms diagram.

Pitcher's Choice

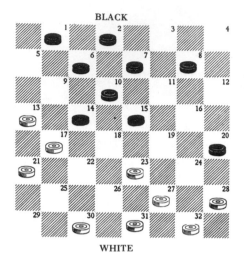

BLACK

WHITE

Problem No. 98
From Game Opening 12-16, 22-18, 16-19
By Walter Hellman
BLACK: 1, 2, 6, 7, 8, 10, 14, 15, 20
WHITE: 13, 17, 21, 23, 27, 28, 30, 31, 32

Black to play and draw

Solution

15-18—A, 30-25, 7-11, 28-24—B, 8-12, 24-19—C, 11-16, 32-28, 2-7, 19-15, 10-26, 17-3, 26-30, 3-7, 30-26—D, 31-15, 6-9, 13-6, 1-19—E. Drawn.

A—The start of a nice combination by the long-time Three-Move world champion.

B—If 23-19, then 10-15, 19-10, 6-15, 17-10, 18-23, 27-18, 15-29, 10-7, 11-16, 7-3, 8-12, 32-27 (3-8, 20-24), 29-25, 3-8, 25-22, 8-11, 22-18 places the burden on White.

C—Not 32-28 as Black has the waiting 2-7, running White out of moves.

D—The pitch that brings the game to a close with a nice flourish.

E—From: 12-16, 22-18, 16-19, 24-15, 10-19, 23-16, 11-20, 21-17, 7-10, 25-21, 3-7 (the right follow-up), 17-13, 9-14, 18-9, 5-14, 29-25, 8-11 (8-12 is doubtful), 25-22, 11-15, 22-17, 4-8, 26-23. Forms diagram. The late Mr. Hellman had held the modern Three-Move championship far longer than any other player, having played in nine world title matches! He has won six matches, drawn two and lost but one, to Dr. Marion Tinsley.

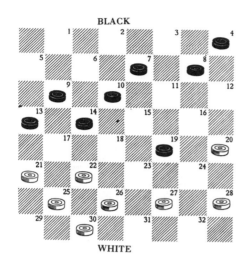

BLACK

WHITE

Problem No. 99

From Game Opening 12-16, 23-18, 16-19

By Dr. Marion F. Tinsley

BLACK: 4, 7, 8, 9, 10, 13, 14, 19

WHITE: 20, 21, 22, 25, 26, 27, 28, 30

White to play and win

Solution

27-23, 8-12, 23-16, 12-19, 20-16, 10-15, 16-12, 14-18, 21-17—A, 7-10, 17-14—A, 10-17, 25-21, 18-25, 21-5—B, 25-29, 5-1, 15-18, 1-6, 18-23, 28-24, 19-28, 26-19, 28-32, 6-10, 13-17, 10-14, 17-21, 19-15—C. In complete control, White wins.

A—These moves enabled Dr. Marion Tinsley to defeat the late Jackson Dworsky in the finals of the 1949 Cedar Point (Ohio) Masters' Tournament.

B—White has the situation well under control and proceeds to wrap up the game, the heat, the tourney and the championship. Many years later, 1974, Dr. Tinsley won the 'big four'—the National, the Southern, Cedar Point and the Florida Masters, . . . Checkerdom's Grand Slam.

C—From: 12-16, 23-18, 16-19, 24-15, 10-19, 18-15 (best), 11-18, 22-15, 7-10 (7-11 is standard), 25-22, 9-13, 29-25, 5-9, 27-24, 9-14, 32-27, 8-12, 24-20, 3-8, 27-23, 2-7, 23-16, 12-19, 31-26, 6-9 (loses 14-18, 20-16, 18-23, 27-18, 8-11, draws), 15-6, 1-10. Forms diagram.

Brooklyn Dodger

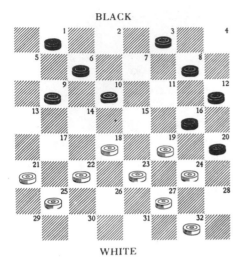

BLACK

WHITE

Problem No. 100
From Game Opening 12-16, 24-19,
8-12
By Mike Lieber
BLACK: 1, 3, 6, 8, 9, 10, 12, 16, 20
WHITE: 18, 19, 21, 22, 23, 24, 25,
    27, 32
White to play and draw

Solution

18-15—A, 9-13, 22-18—A, 3-7, 25-22—A, 7-11, 22-17!—B, 13-22, 18-14, 10-17, 21-14, 15-22, 14-10, 6-15, 23-14, 16-23, 27-4, 20-27, 32-23—C. Drawn.

A—White appears to be cramped and running out of moves, but these moves lead to an instructive and clean-cut draw.

B—The combination White had in mind at Note A and saves the entire variation. The 'Brooklyn Stroke' idea.

C—From: 12-16, 24-19, 8-12, 22-18, 10-14, 25-22, 4-8, 22-17, 9-13, 18-9, 13-22, 26-17, 6-22, 30-25, 22-26, 31-22, 7-10, 22-18, 2-6, 28-24, 16-20, 25-22, 5-9, 29-25, 11-16. Forms diagram.

The American Checker Federation

This is the parent body that conducts and sponsors all U.S.A. National Tournaments, as well as many state and local events.

30 The End?

Although an end has come to our pages, there is no end to the wonderful world of Checkers. For hundreds of years the devotees of Dama, patron goddess of Checkers, have sought the secrets of her mysterious enchantment. Yet even today, as ever, she still evokes the words of the poet: "Age cannot wither her, nor custom stale / Her infinite variety."

To that infinite variety, our book is but a humble introduction. Through its pages we have endeavored to entertain and instruct. But our fondest hope is that we have opened for the beginner new portals upon a scene where "every prospect pleases."

In yet another sense this page is not the end. Because what we further recommend is that you go back to the beginning. Review each position and each game. You will be surprised at the new revelations that emerge as you achieve increased insight and understanding of checker principles.

We recommend also that you obtain other books on Checkers, books in which the masters reveal their best games and advice. Add to this lore the experience you gain by playing strong opponents, and you will see how rapidly your crossboard prowess improves.

And if we have succeeded in giving you some hint of the beauty of Checkers, if we have encouraged you to explore its offerings further—then the end of this book can indeed be a beginning for you. So take it from here!

Index